Mudlarks
and the
Silent Highwayman

an illustrated novelette by Alan M. Clark

More books by Alan M. Clark

Art Books

Alan M. Clark, The Paint in My Blood, Illustration & Fine Art
(full-color)

Pain and Other Petty Plots to Keep You in Stitches
(monochrome)

Bastards and Guttersnipes, The Neglected Children of Alan M. Clark, Studies and Interior Illustrations, Volumes I & II
(monochrome)

Novels

A Parliament of Crows

The Door that Faced West

The Surgeons Mate: A Dismemoir
(tangential to the Jack the Ripper Victims Series)

Siren Promised
(a collaboration with Jeremy Robert Johnson)

D.D. Murphry, Secret Policeman
(a collaboration with Elizabeth Massie)

Novel Series
Jack the Ripper Victims Series

Of Thimble and Threat

Say Anything but Your Prayers

A Brutal Chill in August

Apologies to the Cat's Meat Man

The Prostitute's Price

13 Miller's Court
(a collaboration with John Linwood Grant)

Blood of Father Time Series

The Blood of Father Time: The New Cut

The Blood of Father Time: The Mystic Clan's Grand Plot
(collaborations with Stephen C. Merritt, and Lorelei Shannon)

Praise for the writing of Alan M. Clark

"Crime and horror wrapped in a wondrous symmetry, made all the more terrifying by its factual basis, *A Parliament of Crows* has it all. Read it!"
—F. Paul Wilson, author of Cold City

"In a publishing landscape where everything has been done...to death, comes something marvelous, frightening, and new--*The Surgeon's Mate: A Dismemoir*. Alan M. Clark has birthed a masterpiece that oscillates between bone-deep confessional and hide-your-eyes-horror."
—Charles Atkins author of The Prodigy

"*Of Thimble and Threat* is a terrifically absorbing read. A mature novel and superbly researched. The image of silver in the blood was woven expertly and made the ending luminous and poignant."
—Simon Clark, author of *Vampyrrhic* and *Night of the Triffids*

"Clark proves himself to be the ultimate double-threat, his prose every bit as evocative and compelling as his art. Steeped in Victoriana *Say Anything but Your Prayers* is a worthy edition to Ripperology."
—Steven Savile, author of *Silver* and *London Macabre*

"In *Jack the Ripper Victim Series: The Double Event*, Clark's attention to details of the era reveals a class system where a poor woman alone is all but doomed to an early grave. Readers will come away touched by these profound portraits of desperate women and shocked by not just the crimes which ended in their demise, but the greater crimes of a society that offered them no hope. This book is a must-read; be prepared to be horrified."
—Nancy Kilpatrick
Author: The Power of the Blood series
Editor: *Danse Macabre* and *Expiration Date*

From the review of *A Butal Chill in August* in *Ripperologist Magazine*:
Everything about this novel inspires admiration. It reveals terrible things about the world of London's poor, yet it is a work of great beauty, ceaselessly entertaining and compellingly readable. The rigging of a ship burning in the fire at the London Docks 'sparkles like a spider web dripping with dew at sunrise'. When we finally meet Jack the Ripper, he emerges from the darkness like an ordinary man, smelling of sulphur and soap. *A Brutal Chill in August* is a triumph.

From the review of *Apologies to the Cat's Meat Man* in *Ripperologist Magazine*:
Alan M. Clark is not the first author to find the victims' lives irresistible, but he has no equal when it comes to writing vivid and intellectually provocative stories about them. This is storytelling of the highest quality.

IFD Publishing
P.O. Box 40776, Eugene Oregon, 97404
www. Ifdpublishing.com

Mudlarks and the Silent Highwayman
Copyright © 2020 by Alan M. Clark

All rights reserved. No part of this book may be reproduced or transmitted in any form or by any means, electronic or mechanical, including photocopying, recording, or by any information storage and retrieval system, without the written consent of the publisher, except where permitted by law.

This is a work of fiction. Although it is inspired by historical settings, the characters have been created for the sake of this story and are either products of the author's imagination or are used fictitiously. Any resemblance to actual events or locales or persons, living or dead, is entirely coincidental.

"The Silent Highwayman" Cartoon from *Punch* magazine July, 1858

The girl in the illustration on pages 53 and 64 is inspired by the one in the painting "Locked in the Angel Closet," an acrylic collaboration created by Jill Bauman and Alan M. Clark.

The ship in the illustration on page 59 is inspired in part by the one in the painting "Well Done Condor" by Charles Dixon, which depicts one of the vessels involved in the British naval bombardment of Alexandria in 1882.

"Monster Soup commonly called Thames Water" Coloured etching by W. Heath, 1828.

"Dirty Father Thames" Cartoon and accompanying poem from *Punch* magazine October, 1848

"The Wonders of a London Water Drop" Cartoon from *Punch* magazine May, 1850

"Faraday giving his card to Father Thames; And we hope the Dirty Fellow will consult the learned Professor" Cartoon from *Punch* magazine July, 1855

"Father Thames Introducing His Offspring to the Fair City of London. (A Design for a Fresco in the New Houses of Parliament.)" engraving by John Leech. Cartoon from *Punch* magazine July, 1858

"How Dirty Old Father Thames was Whitewashed" Cartoon from *Punch* magazine July, 1858

ISBN: 978-1-7342978-4-3
Printed in the United States of America

Thanks to:
Bill and Joan Clark
Melody Clark
Jill Bauman
Mark Roland
Lisa Snellings
David Conover
Cynthia Drewek
Carol Clark-Evans
Mad Wilson
Jim Goad
Susie Ballinger
Dianne Buja
John Linwood Grant

Author/Illustrator's Note

I have been immersed in the history of Victorian London for nearly a decade while writing the Jack the Ripper Victims Series, novels about the lives of those killed by the Whitechapel Murderer. In the midst of research for the stories, I discovered all sorts of occupations of the period that involved scavenging and recycling. While that sounds good in the world of today that suffers such destruction from our various wastes, the recycling in Victorian times took a terrible toll on the health of those who did the work. During the Industrial Revolution of the 19th century, jobs were scarce and many achingly poor Londoners became willing to do the worst things in order to earn a crust. Toshers scavenged in the sewers. Bone grubbers collected bones door to door or by going through the rubbish of taverns or households that could afford to serve joints of beef, pork, or mutton. Purefinders collected feces in the streets. Night soil men emptied the human waste from cesspits and privy vaults. This one actually paid well, but because of that, many allowed their vaults and cesspits to overflow before they were willing to pay the price. Mudlarks, mostly children, scavenged the banks of the River Thames, looking for anything that had been lost in the water and might be found at low tide in the exposed area known as the foreshore. Markets existed for nearly all that was collected, yet the returns were paltry considering the time and energy involved and the risks to health.

    A time when the majority of transportation employed horses, the streets were littered with dung and awash in over ten thousand gallons of equine urine each day. That and the leakage from overflowing cesspits and privy vaults found its way into the River Thames when the rains came. As a result, the river reeked.

The people of London recognized that much illness came from the river. The common belief was that illness was born on bad smells—miasma as it was called—and that people became ill when breathing the malodorous air. The city was in fact suffering outbreaks of deadly waterborne illness during a time when much of the science of microbes was still under debate.

I write this during the COVID-19 flu pandemic, and while knowing something of the 1918 Spanish influenza pandemic that infected approximately 500 million people. In comparison, the waterborne epidemics of Victorian London were small events, except to those who suffered through them.

In the back of this volume, the reader will find a short article about the dangers of illness from the Thames in Victorian times, and The Great Stink, a nearly two-month-long period in the summer of 1858, during which those who could afford to do so, evacuated London to get away from the smell coming off the river.

In such periods of fouled water and air, the poor, needing the income, or fearing unemployment, continued to work, despite the dangers of exposure to disease from real or imagined sources.

This is a fanciful story about a mudlark and the choices he made within that environment.

—Alan M. Clark
Eugene, Oregon

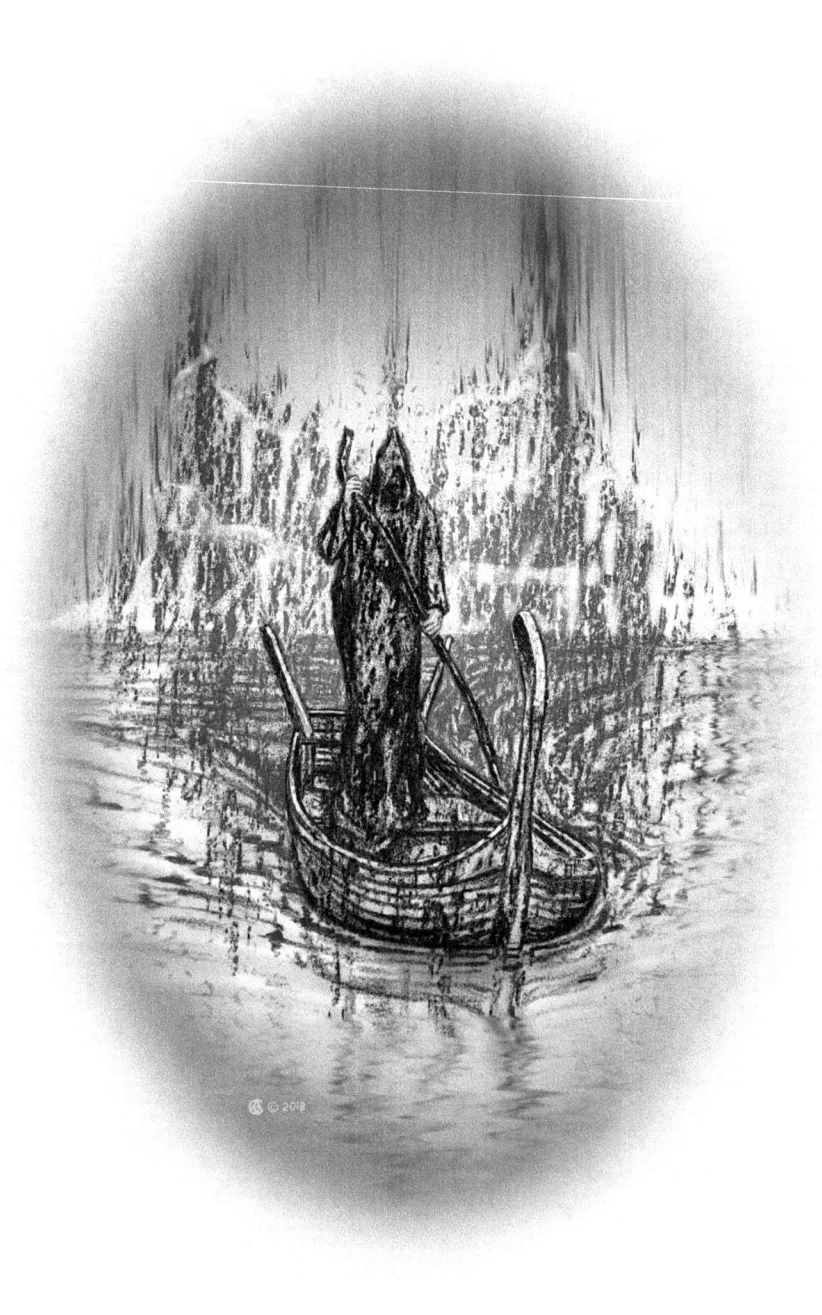

Mudlarks
and the
Silent Highwayman

an illustrated novelette by Alan M. Clark

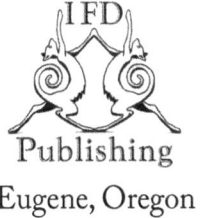

IFD Publishing
Eugene, Oregon

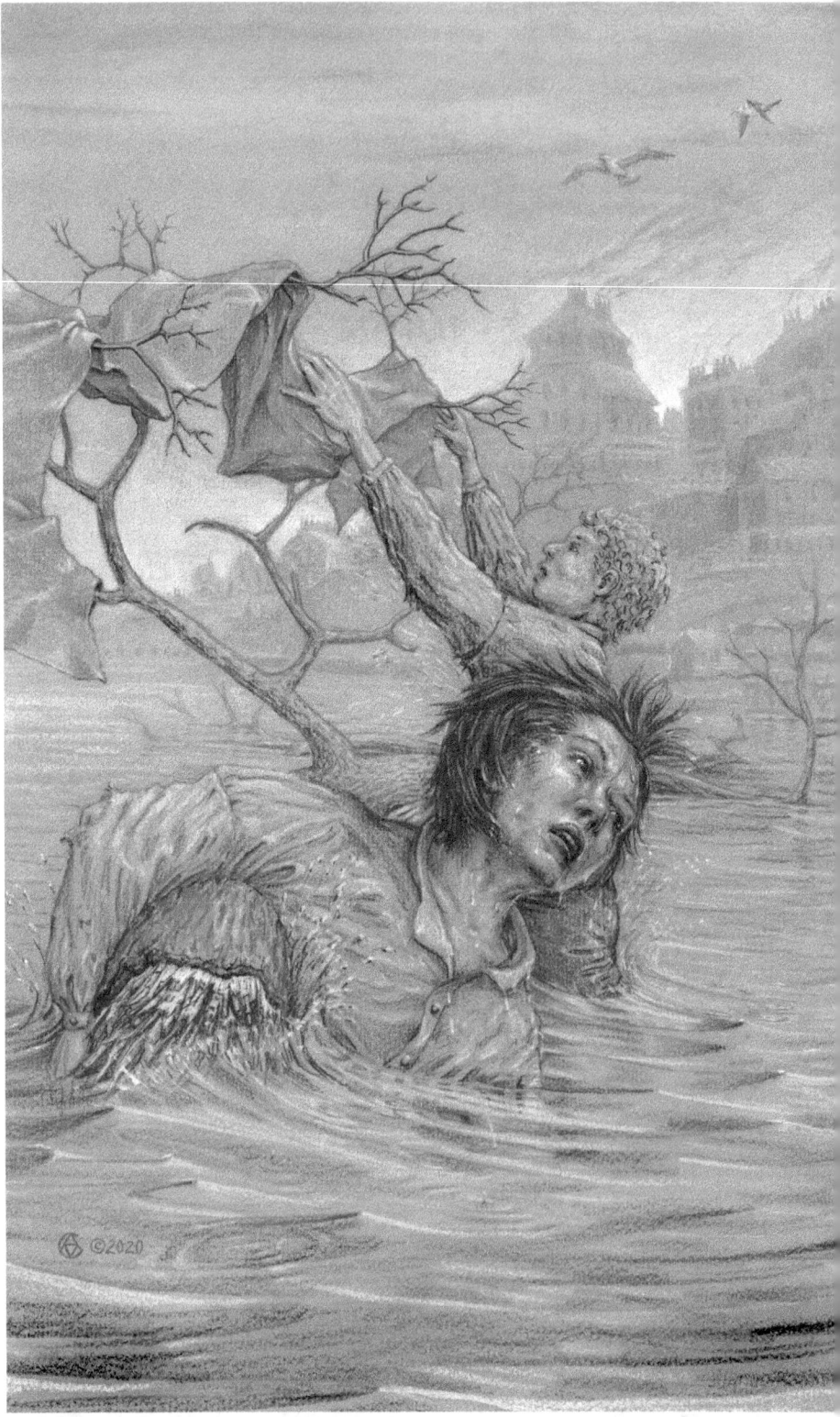

Mudlarks

Limehouse and the Isle of Dogs
October 30, 1884

Half-submerged in the murky River Thames, twelve-year-old Albert Gladwick struggled to keep the fallen tree limb from getting away. His new friend, Turvey, worked to free a long, torn length of blue linen from the branch's twiggy clutches. If they could free it, they'd earn perhaps three pence selling the fabric. Hugging the limb under his right arm and leaning forward, digging his toes into the mud and grit of the river bottom, Albert fought the current that was trying to drag the heavy branch downstream. Though he did his best to ignore his imagination, he couldn't help thinking that unseen creatures moved through the water surrounding him.

Turvey leapt again and again to break the twigs holding the cloth, his splashing about so vigorous the foul water's faint odor of slops rose up around them. Alberts mother, Chelsey, called that smell a *pong*. "It's the foul breath of the grundylows, what live in the water," she'd told him when he was very little. "Bubbles rising from the river, that's their breath. It's how most illness comes into the world. You see that, move swiftly to get away."

The insistent current pulled Albert upright, then backwards until he lost his footing on the river bottom. Feeling something brush along his right hip, he cried out and let go.

Holding onto the fabric, Turvey leaned back, bracing himself to hang on. Albert twisted around and sloshed forward to lend a hand. He hoped the action took him away from whatever might be after him. Before he could assist his friend, the last few twigs holding the cloth broke away and the limb continued moving downstream.

The water calmer, Albert saw nothing but green-brown light twisting in the current. *I don't believe in Grundylows*, he told himself, and turned to the other boy. "You saved us a mad scramble through the water."

Turvey reeled in the sodden linen. His bad eye bulged from its socket as he grinned.

Albert became aware that the weight of the large canvas sack he routinely carried over his shoulder was missing. Its makeshift strap had been loose. Empty but for a piece of roofing lead he'd found earlier, the sack had surely gone downriver with the branch. Albert cursed his damnable bad luck, then quickly turned away from the thought.

"A good thing one of us can hold fast," Turvey said with a scoffing laugh.

Though they'd known each other a mere two days, Albert had got used to his friend's jeering remarks. "Right, I can't keep a grip on much today—lost my sack in the fight."

"Serves you right."

Albert swallowed the insults that collected on his tongue—none of them had been clever enough. A rather earnest child, he wasn't practiced at the good-natured jibes his friend enjoyed. He'd work on that. In the meantime, all he could do was to take the abuse in stride.

"Badly stained," Turvey said, "but not much rot." He shook water from the blue fabric, folded it roughly, and placed it in his own collection sack, which was more of a leather bucket with small holes punched in it to allow liquid to flow out.

The boys slogged their way back to the bank where they'd been sitting when they first spied the cloth in the branch floating by.

"Since we both spotted it about the same time," Albert said, "it's only fair we share what it earns."

"You did your best, I suppose," Turvey said with a smirk.

Despite the loss of the canvas sack, Albert had enjoyed having the help and the companionship, something he rarely had in scavenging. "What if we got the others—all of us scavengers—to search the river together, then shared the profits of what we found? We'd do better than we each do alone, guarding our secrets."

Turvey screwed up his face, glared at Albert with his one good eye. "Start with that and you'll see Hardly's family taking charge," he said. "Our freedom will be gone. There'll be those seeking favor and we'll end up with quotas hard to meet. That's what the guttersnipes as run with kidsmen suffer. You want to go up against George Hardly, or worse, each day?"

George Hardly caused no end of trouble along the north bank near Limehouse. He was tall for his thirteen years, skeletally thin, yet strong; a cruel boy with a burn scar making a knotty burl out of the cheek on the right side of his face. Stories went about that his father, a tosher and bone grubber, regularly beat him with a leather strap, and had disfigured the boy's face while in a drunken rage.

A week earlier, Hardly had snuck up on Albert, swept his legs out from under him, kicked him in the gut, and taken a modest find: the half-rotten remains of a mongrel. Unable to get up, Albert had writhed in pain in the sand and gravel. Hardly leaned over him, put his scowling, scarred face too close to Albert's. "Won't be long," he growled, "you want to search this part of the river, you'll all be work-

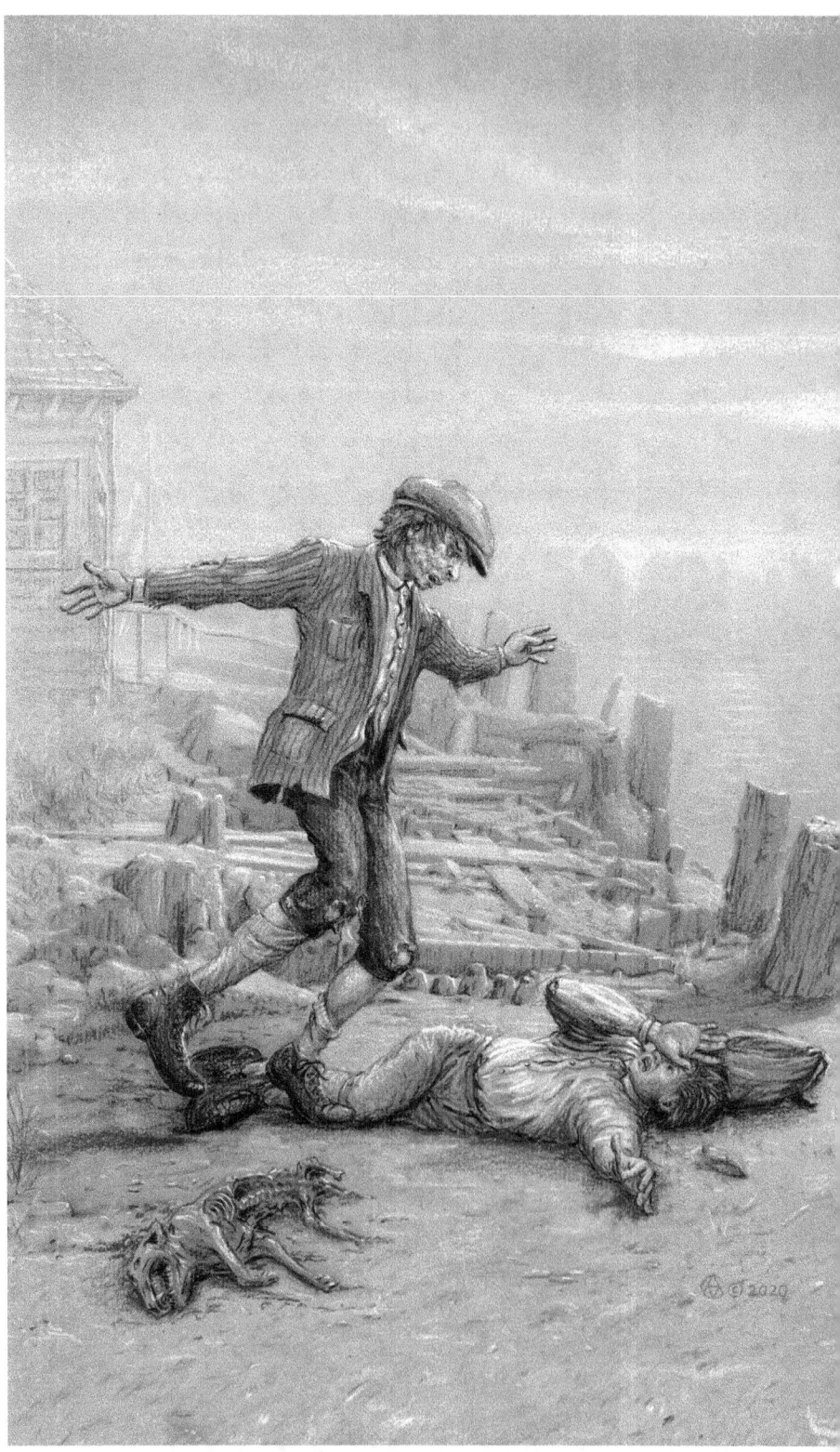

ing for me. I'll get a piece of everything you and the others find."

Albert kept a wary eye out to avoid further contact with the bully boy. Just the day before, he'd experienced a withering feeling in his gut—an echo of the pain the older boy had inflicted—as Hardly's eyes found him from some distance away along the foreshore. Engaged in threatening another boy at the time, the bully hadn't followed as Albert fled, climbing the bank toward the street.

Hardly did not own that part of the river yet, but it seemed only a matter of time before he did. He had older brothers who plundered barges in the night and sold the stolen goods through local *family people*.

"No," Turvey continued, "we're better off going our separate ways so the Hardly's can't keep up." He pulled the blue linen cloth from his leather bucket, spread it out, and folded it in half more carefully.

Albert could see what he meant, and nodded his agreement, yet that must not have been enough.

"You have some foolish notions," Turvey said, pulling out a clasp knife.

Albert stepped back, thinking he'd lost his share of the cloth and his new friend.

"Goodwill is fine for the well-to-do," Turvey said. "I need a mate what's hard enough to defend his own." He cut the cloth with the knife along the fold, handed one half to Albert, then turned and walked off with the other.

Dumbfounded, yet relieved their disagreement hadn't come to blows or worse, Albert watched him go. Then outrage made him call out, "We'd've got more selling it in one piece."

Turvey didn't respond.

I'd have done better to insult him more.

Friends and loyalties were difficult on the banks of the Thames.

Mostly boys between the ages of seven and fifteen, the Mudlarks were secretive creatures protecting territories, each a solitary sort of child. Like Albert, they were from families one step away from destitution. All the children he knew did some sort of work to contribute income to their family households. Even the children fortunate enough to go to the Ragged Schools did some sort of piecework at night. Among such poor children on the river banks, the competition, good-natured or otherwise, was to be expected.

I should harden my heart if I want more friends. The idea seemed to go against an effort to find and keep companions, but he decided he'd have to consider it even so.

He expected he wouldn't be speaking or spending time with Turvey again for a long while. Already within the year, he'd lost two good friends to fever. A familiar loneliness grew in his breast.

Albert couldn't go home until his clothes had dried some or his mum would know he'd been in the river. He slipped the cloth inside his shirt for safekeeping and made his way along the foreshore. Finding himself headed south on the western edge of the Isle of Dogs, he decided to risk a quick exploration among the rushes growing near the drain for the white lead works, a good spot to check since most of the scavengers avoided the area. While much of the foreshore of the Thames offered a firm gravel or sand surface at low tide, the stretch he presently walked held pockets of deep, thick mud that made progress difficult.

Approaching the structure that supported the drain, he saw an unusual dark shape among the oversized grasses, one that he told himself was likely mere shadow. As he got close enough to see between the foliage, the doubt protecting him from unreasonable hope began to fall away. Indeed, the shape held true form and mass—he'd found the wreck of a clinker-built wherry, much like the one his father had once piloted to carry fares up and down, to and fro, along the Thames when he was a waterman.

Pushing the long leaves out of his way, Albert made out the shapes of several crates, a metal chest, and a firkin, all held fast in the mud within the wherry.

Though he wanted to shout for joy, he knew better than to draw attention to the find. Instead, he stood holding his head, his heart thumping giddily in his chest. Plainly, the boat had sat unnoticed for a while, lying on its side, half-buried in the silt among the rushes. He imagined the vessel got free during recent wind storms, possibly at night while no one was watching. In his mind's eye, he saw it wander down-stream beneath dim, flickering stars until it fetched up on the foreshore beside him.

How might he present the possible treasure trove to his mother without her knowing where it came from?

That he did not have her permission to work the river had always rankled. "It's too dangerous," she'd said the first time he'd brought it up. "The grundylows don't just spread disease—they like to pull children down. You want to be the next to go missing, turn up drowned?"

Albert had told Turvey what his mother said. He'd laughed. "They're not grundylows! They're grindylows. The mums of all scavengers tell that tall tale to keep their children from the water's edge." Turvey shook his head, giggling. "You *are* a gulpy one."

"I didn't say I believed!"

"You needn't have done. I've seen the way you look at the water."

That forced Albert to reason it out. If there were such creatures drowning mudlarks, Turvey would have gone missing long ago. Albert had never seen anyone so willing to venture out into the river.

With all that, he still imagined the creatures just beneath the glare on the rippling surface whenever he dangled his legs close to the water, or while wading out into it.

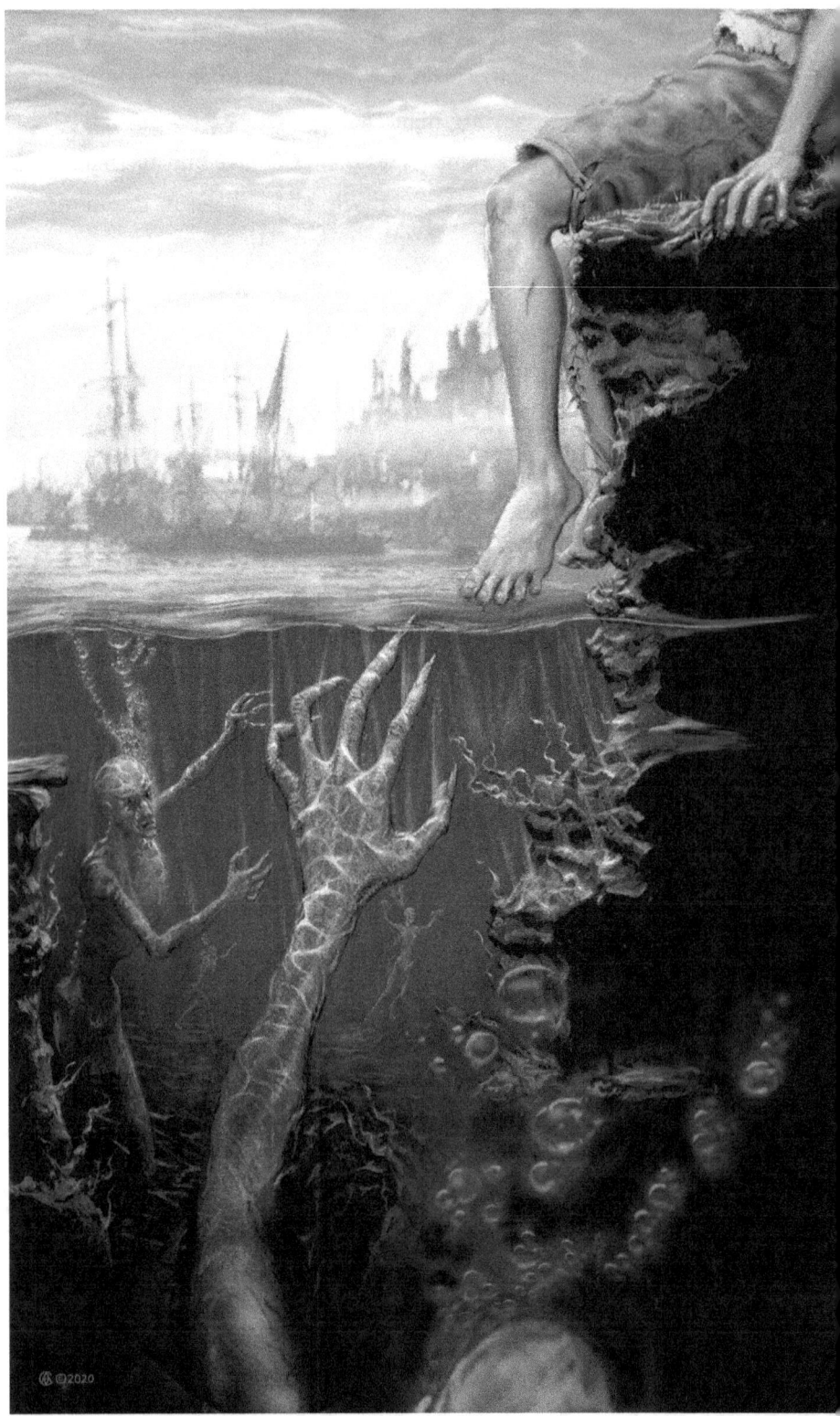

Despite the childish fears, Albert was simply drawn to the water and scavenging. The possibility of finding unexpected reward held his interest like nothing else had in his short life. And ever since his father had run off, a year past, Albert had thought he should make decisions for himself about how to earn. After all, he would soon be a man.

Knowing how much Papa's departure had hurt her, Albert didn't want to challenge his mum or bring further grief by disappointing her, so he'd kept his activities at the river a secret.

He knew what she'd say: "You'll be charged as a thief!"

Yet here he'd made a real find, at long last—valuable goods, gold, jewels perhaps!

Albert pried at the crates trying to get them open.

The landlord hasn't been paid in almost a month. She knows we must take every chance to earn. Yet I must know what I've found before I say anything, or she'll become cross with me. If it's worth enough, if it's wonderful, Mum'll have a change of heart.

The lids to the crates were nailed down tight.

"Bloody butt and six toes," he cursed aloud. Then, fearing that someone might have heard, he calmed himself and looked up and down the foreshore. Though he saw no one nearby, he crouched lower amidst the rushes and felt himself sink further into the mud.

He abandoned the crates in favor of the metal chest. That, he decided, was the most promising container. The thing was a foot square and half a foot deep. Trying unsuccessfully to open it, he found a keyhole and decided it was locked. That meant it indeed held something valuable. He wiped some of the grit and mud from its surface. Seeing that where exposed, the metal gleamed brightly, he stopped.

How might he keep it concealed while carrying it? He thought that heaping more mud on the chest would help disguise the shape, but anyone seeing him would know he carried a large object. Though he'd be able to lift the heavy box, he couldn't run with it if spotted.

Likewise the crates and firkin would be heavy and stand out if he tried to carry them away. Too bad he'd lost his heavy canvas sack in the fight with the tree limb. He needed to get the containers open and find a new sack to put things in, one he could dirty up and throw over his shoulder. A shapeless thing like that—no one would suspect he carried anything of value. The only other sack he had big enough hung on a hook back at the lodgings.

With the shadows grown long, Albert knew the hour had become late. He didn't have what he needed to open the containers and reveal his treasure, let alone haul it all away with him.

He sat back and surveyed the scene again. Resting high on the foreshore beside the drain, surrounded with dense orange rushes, and hidden within the deepening shadows, the wherry wasn't easy to spot. With the unusual color of the plants, and a fear that the drain exhausted poisons into the river, most of the scavengers, including George Hardly, avoided the area.

The coming high tide wasn't likely to dislodge any of the find from the mud's tight grip, yet Albert had small hope that the wherry would remain hidden for long. Eventually, even if Hardly didn't find it, someone on nearby Hutching's Wharf would see the wreck and investigate, or another river scavenger unconcerned about the drain would stumble upon the site. Albert would return with a lantern to aid his salvage in the dark, but feared that would only draw attention to the find.

No, he had to go home. Mum would be in their lodgings in Narrow Street, preparing a meal with what little they had. The salvage would have to wait until morning. Hopefully, no one would stumbled upon it in the night.

Albert pulled his feet from the sucking mud. Placing them on the firmest patches of the foreshore, he made his way north toward home. One misplaced step found his left leg penetrating the muck half-way to the buttoned knee of his breeches. He wriggled and tugged it loose, and kept moving.

Filthy and panting heavily in the chill autumn air, Albert arrived at the shadows under the West India Docks Pier. He was relieved to find his shoes, socks, and jacket still in the spot where he'd hidden them; a hole beneath a collapsed stone stairway that began at the base of the eroded embankment. Though his shoes had become hopelessly ragged—holes in their soles and the right one missing its heel—another scavenger would gladly take them. The leather alone could be sold to makers of Prussian-blue pigment.

Mr. Halpert, the marine store dealer, would buy almost any common item found along the river, if only for a tiny sum. He'd take anything made of metal, any type of bone, any spun or woven materials, as long as the items weren't too rotten. Those who made fertilizer would buy items of paper, wood, or small dead animals.

Albert took the easiest route back to street-level, a steep erosion seam, worn into the crumbling bank by weather and the passage of countless others like him.

Seeing Thomas Conway standing near the cast iron bridge of the pier, Albert hid behind a stack of containers. Not wanting the bother of talking to the boy, he would wait for him to turn and look away before crossing the road.

The tow-headed child, a year younger than Albert, stood about five feet from the where the bridge met the river bank at the end of Cuba Street. Thomas craned his neck as if looking for someone. He seemed unaware that he was in the way, as a group of merchants moved around him. One of the gentlemen smacked him on the back of the head as he went by. Thomas stumbled under the blow and ran into a laborer carrying a heavy coil of cable. The man shoved the boy to one side, nearly knocking him down. The lad took the rough treatment without complaint.

New to the river banks and green, the younger boy was a nuisance. His clothing—gray woolen jacket, blue cotton shirt, brown woolen breeches, and gray socks—though worn and patched many times over, didn't look ragged. His brown shoes had been carefully repaired with pieces of black leather. Someone looked out for the boy.

"Where's the best place to search for valuables," Thomas had asked on the day they'd met.

"Salvage turns up most anywhere along the river," Albert said, with an indefinite wave toward the water. "The thing is to be the first to find it. Take care not to anger the others with prying questions."

The advice did little good. The younger boy tried to befriend and question all the other scavengers in a similar way. He had purple bruises and a black eye after approaching George Hardly. Then, Thomas's father, a frightening Irishman who earned writing gallows ballads, came to the river and set the scavengers straight on how his son should be treated.

Thereafter, none of the boys, nor the few girls who scavenged the river, would talk to Thomas. All, that is, except for Albert, and he made certain no one saw him speak to the lad.

When Thomas finally turned and looked away, Albert slipped from behind the containers and hurried into Cuba Street, mixing with those walking beside the warehouse to his right. He thought he'd got by unnoticed.

No such luck. "Albert!" Thomas cried. Something about his tone suggested he'd found the one he sought.

Albert stopped, looked around, saw no one of any concern watching. He walked back around to the western wall of the warehouse and faced the river as the boy approached.

Thomas held a single leaf torn from a newspaper or a magazine between two of his grubby fingers, as if he didn't want to hold the page tightly. A breeze tried to snatch the paper away. With a grimace of reluctance, he added more fingers to his grip.

"My mother give me this. It's from *Punch*. It's old, but she says he's still on the river, looking to nail children, and take them to the underworld."

Albert looked at the illustration on the yellowing, wrinkled page. The engraving depicted a phantom in the form of a cloaked skeleton, rowing a boat on the river. Dead animals bobbed on the nearby surface of the water. "Looks a bit like Hardly, does he?"

"You don't think…?" Thomas asked, his eyes wide with fear.

"No," Albert chuckled to hear the boy take the suggestion seri-

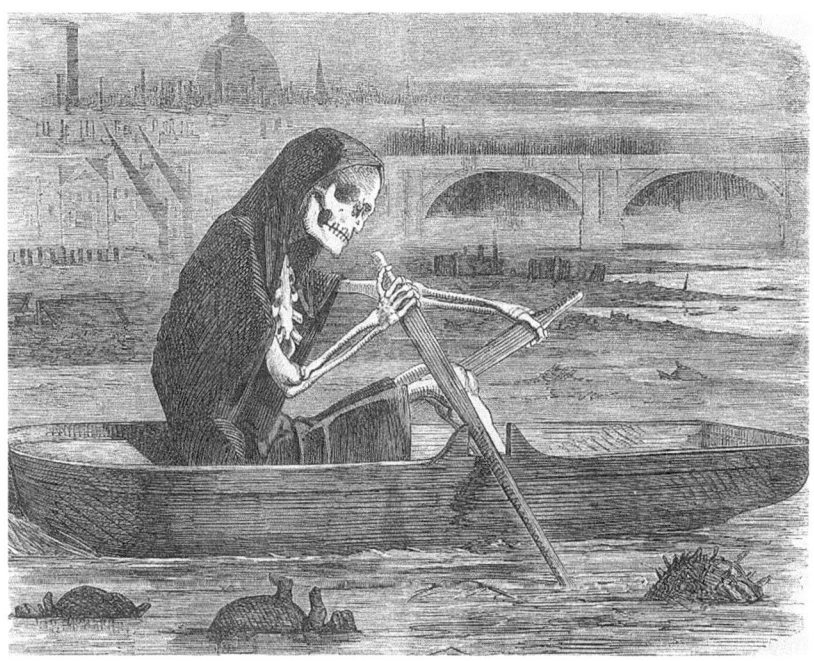

ously. "What are the words beneath the picture," he asked, embarrassed to reveal he couldn't read.

"'The Silent Highwayman: Your Money or your Life.'" Thomas's dirt-smudged brow furrowed with concern.

"He the ghost of a waterman?" Albert thought about his father, presumed dead.

"No, he's not like us—never lived among us—an evil on the water, is all. Mother says he puts the bad smells in the river, the ones what make illness. Then he harvests the children as die, takes them away with him."

That sounded something like what Mum had said about illnesses.

Albert's father, Albert Senior or just Papa, had talked about a ferryman of the dead, named Charon. Papa's mother, whose family had come from Greece, had filled him full of ancient Greek tales that he shared with young Albert. "Belief in Charon is old," he'd said. "My mum thought him mere fancy. But serving in the Royal Navy in the Mediterranean, I met some who still believe we cross over a river to reach the afterlife. Told one fellow I'd been a waterman and he looked at me like he were seeing a ghost, had no more to do with me after that."

With his father's dread description of the gaunt Charon, Albert had found a fear of one day meeting up with the ferryman. Since his father had abandoned the family, Albert tried not to think about the things he'd said.

Thomas's picture of the Silent Highwayman, had resurrected the foreboding, and Albert got a chill.

Since beginning his work of mucking about in the river, he'd become ill numerous times, mostly ailments of the gut, yet he'd also had sore eyes and skin, strange rashes, and cuts on his feet, legs, and hands that had swelled with corruption and given him fevers before slowly healing. He'd succeeded in hiding most of that from Mum.

Albert looked out on the water for the Silent Highwayman, glanced around the vicinity of the pier again to make certain they weren't watched. George Hardly stood out in the water two hundred yards away, poking around the weed and refuse caught up on the stump of a rotten dolphin.

Turning back to Thomas, Albert saw the boy's eyes brimmed, tears glistening, ready to fall.

Is he truly so fearful?

"She doesn't want me to work the river," Thomas said. "I-I don't *want* to believe her."

Thomas's mother didn't want him working the foreshore no doubt for the same reasons Mum didn't want Albert doing it: the risks of disease and accidents. And Thomas's mother was trying to dissuade her son with fear, much the way Mum had tried to scare Albert. Mum knew nothing of the dangers of the likes of Hardly. Albert had told her he worked as a pure finder, collecting dog shit from the streets for the Rouel Tannery in Bermondsey.

"Do *you* believe he's on the river?" Thomas asked, waving the illustration in his hand. He gave an impression he might not want the answer. "Have you heard anyone say?"

Albert wanted to point to Hardly—still poking around the rotten dolphin—and say, *He's the one you should worry about.* Instead, he decided he should try having a hard heart. Thomas's fear of the phantom might keep him off the river. "A word or two…"

Thomas's look of concern deepened and his eyes grew wide. He let go the magazine page. The paper flipped over and lifted on the breeze, floating around the corner of the warehouse.

The younger boy turned the corner too, and ran away from the river along Cuba Street.

The page danced upward through the hazy air, flying northward. Though Albert had a chuckle watching the boy run, he didn't like encouraging Thomas's fear.

Mum had done the same to him, putting the grundylows in his head. Whether the fears were well-founded or pure fancy, Albert did have a feeling that something more terrible than George Hardly made sinister mischief along the river.

Occupied with his dark thoughts, he sat, brushed most of the remaining mud from his feet and legs, donned his tattered socks and raggedy shoes, and trudged home.

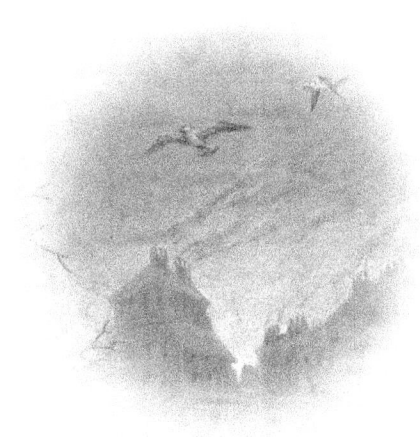

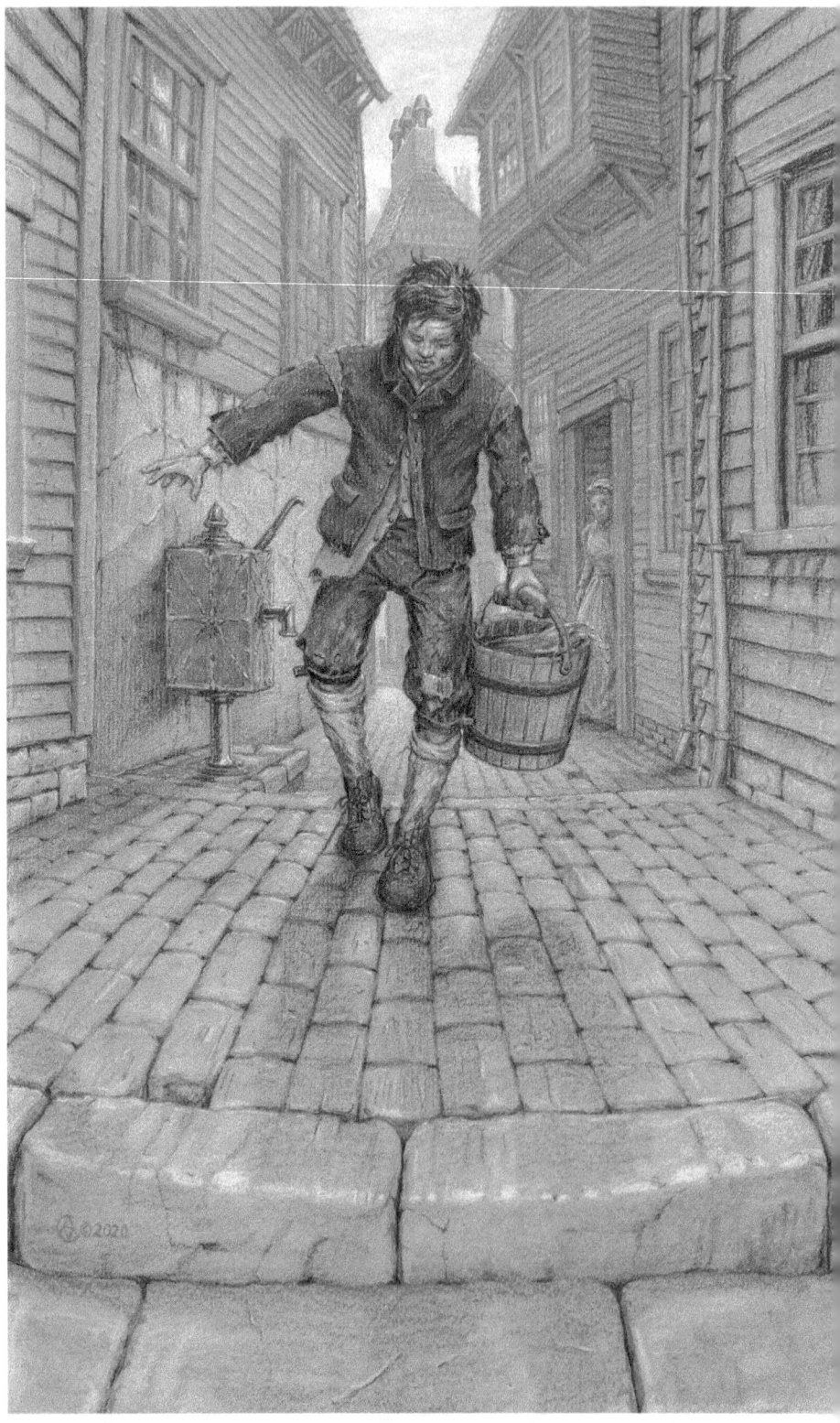

The Eve of Cholera

Mum was up and down in the night many times to use the chamber pot. Trying to sleep in the bed next to her, while full of excitement over the hope of the salvage, Albert got little rest.

In the morning, to his frustration, he found himself attending Mum in her illness.

"I am expected to deliver my collection to the Tannery's man this morning," he told her.

"Before you go, fetch water for me," she said.

Seeing that they were indeed out of fresh water, Albert winced, but dutifully picked up the bucket and went out. The closest public pump was in the passage to White's Rents. He ran there, about a quarter mile, then wobbled his way back home along the stone streets as fast as possible, trying not to spill.

Mum drank deeply of the water upon his return. "You must steady me to the privy and wait to aid my return," she said. "I've become light in the head, and fear a fall."

She remained in the crooked wooden privy behind their lodgings long enough that he might have run to the wreck of the wherry and returned. Not that that would have given him the time he needed, but the thought fed his frustration. Just as he considered making his excuses and leaving her to fend for herself, she stepped out and

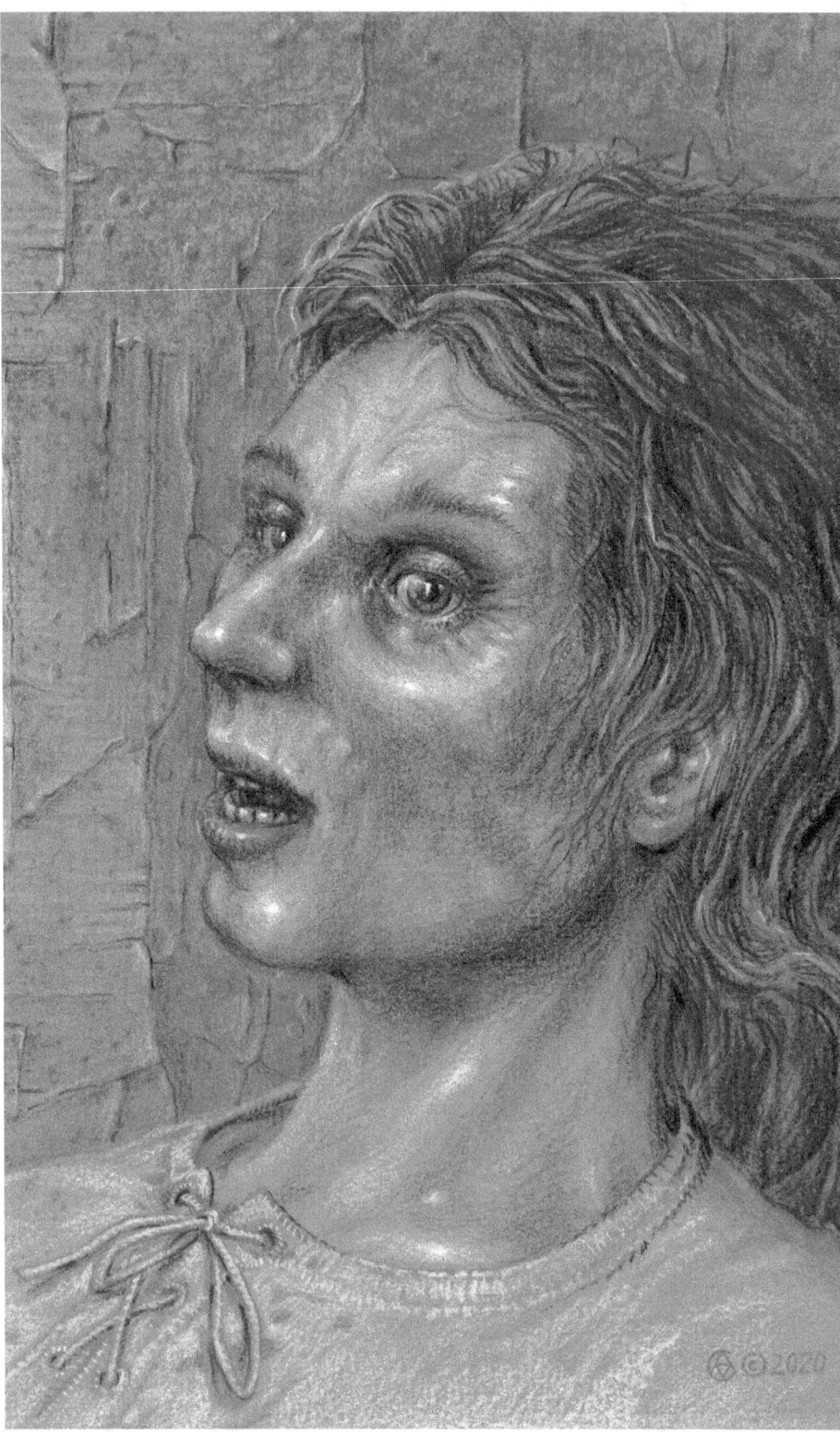

grasped his steadying arm.

Over the next few hours, he found no reasonable excuse to leave her without admitting his goal and revealing that he scavenged the river.

Mum was in a desperate state. He continued to fetch and tote for her through the afternoon, as she had little strength to do for herself. She moaned and writhed, complained of muscle cramps, and retched to no effect in the basin several times. When she lay back on the bed, to his alarm, he saw a rapid pulsing of the vessels in her neck.

"Shall I get someone to help?" he asked, "Aunt Gert is on my way to meet the man what pays for my findings. I could tell her to come help you." If he got away from his mother, he might look in on his find. Aunt Gertrude lived in a room in Tooke Street on the Isle of Dogs, very close to the wrecked wherry. At the least, he could go to the marine store—not nearly as far away—and sell his half of the linen cloth he and Turvey had found.

"Your findings will not go bad. The tannery can wait. Aunt Gertrude has her own problems, and I need you."

Albert felt ashamed of himself for trying so hard to deceive his mother.

Although he had seen Mum looking rough when ill before, he'd never feared her beauty would not return as he did presently. Her rich auburn hair was plastered to her head with perspiration, dark circles grew under her beautiful eyes, and her soft skin looked increasingly pale and gray. Albert didn't know what to do for her. He grudgingly accepted her need to have him nearby.

"If Papa were here—" With the thought of his father, anger welled up, cutting off his words.

The strain lifted from Mum's features for a moment. "He would give me that *smile* of his," she said in a wistful, dreaming voice. "Oh, how he could grin."

Papa had used his winning smile on her every time she caught him in a lie or he failed to do his part and disappointed her.

Albert Gladwick senior had been a good father before he went off to the war. Young Albert recalled that on his seventh birthday he and Papa had made a climb into a church tower to get above the incessant coal smoke haze and view the stars. His father had carried him most of the way up on his shoulders. On that magical night, they'd seen green wisps of the northern lights. "Rare, that is," Papa had said with a warm smile, "a gift given only to good boys."

At present, Albert remembered that event as the happiest moment of his life.

Because watermen had many of the skills required to crew ships—knowledge of piloting among currents, anticipating tides, and dealing with changes in weather—the Royal Navy had pressed many of them into service during the Anglo-Egyptian war, Albert Senior among them.

If Papa had died in Egypt, he thought, *at least I'd have the memory of who he'd been. He made that all a lie.*

Missing a leg, mustered out of the Royal Navy with no pension, and tormented by experiences of which he spoke only cryptically, Papa had become a bitter, broken man, good for nothing. He could not go back to work on the river. Young Albert had done for him while Albert senior drank away the household funds. In addition to the charring work she did by day, Mum had taken to selling matches, flowers, and pencils on the street at night to help keep the family fed. Some nights she'd be out until dawn, trying to earn.

"Common tail, you've become," Papa said one morning when she came home. "I know how you earn. Don't try to tell me differ-

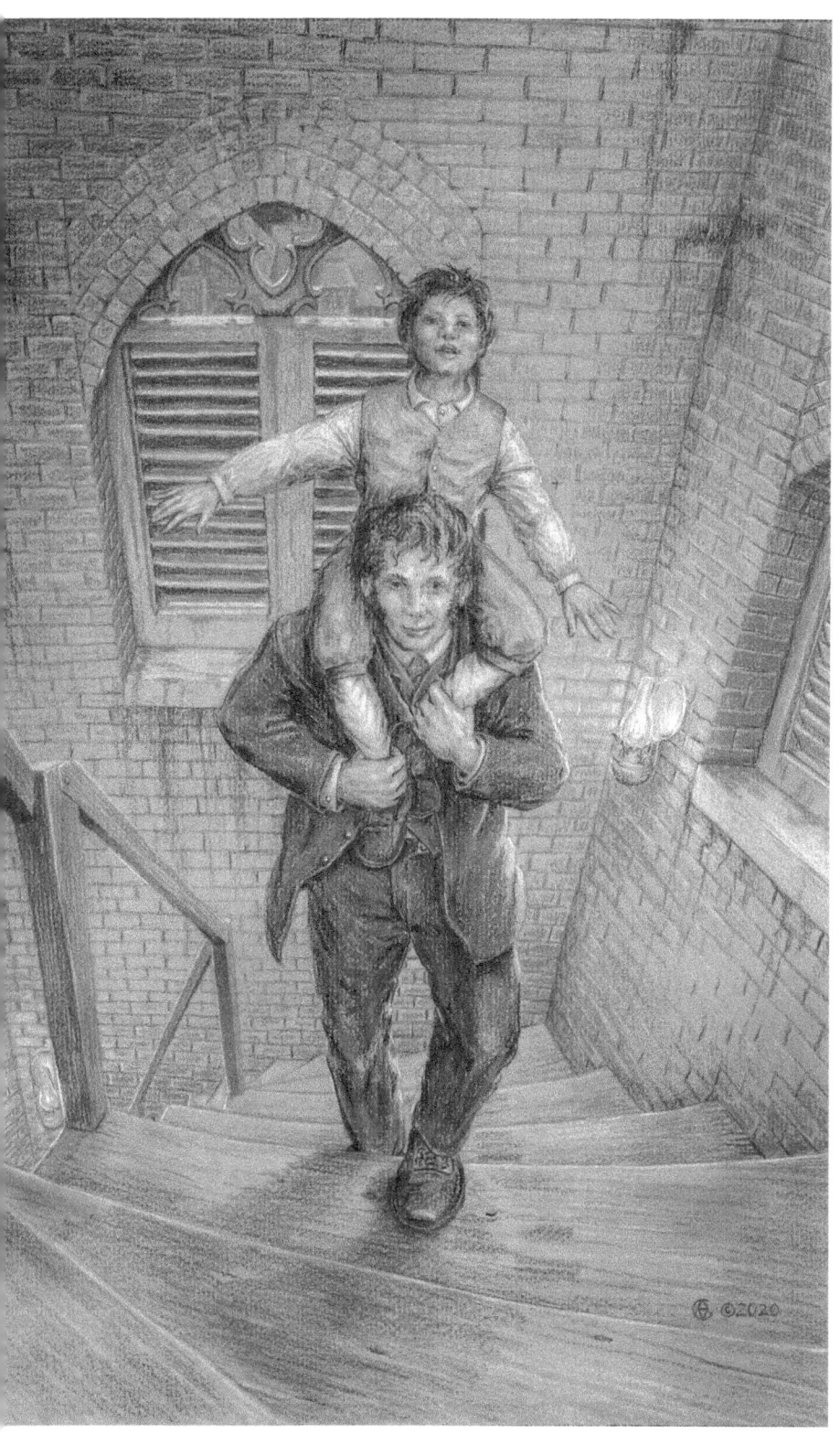

ent."

He raised a hand to strike her and young Albert grabbed his wrist. Albert senior wrenched the hand loose and backhanded him with it. The boy fell, struck his head on the bed rail, and began to cry.

"If you *were* my son," Papa said, his sweating, unkempt face a fright to look upon, "you wouldn't weep so easily."

Albert ceased to cry, and stared at his father's crazed features, not understanding.

Papa had a brief look of shame, said sadly, "You'd be better off if I crossed the river." Then he'd fled the room.

That had been over a year ago. Papa had never come back.

Albert didn't look for his father in South London. He didn't think the Thames was the river he'd meant.

If Papa still lived, having but one leg, his prospects were poor. If he'd been whole, Albert could have imagined all sorts of reasons for his disappearance. Men went missing from London all the time. No, if Papa had not died, he'd become lost on the streets or somewhere in the relief system.

Albert's sadness for the loss of his father had slowly turned to anger.

What had he meant to say to Mum about Papa? "If he were here, *willing* to do his part…," Albert began anew.

"The illness will pass," Mum said with a stern look.

He knew that if Albert Gladwick senior stood before them in that moment, she would defend him and his worst deeds, still smitten as she was with his smile.

In his disgust at the thought, Albert nearly walked out to return to the wherry.

But then Mum looked him in the eye, said, "I have *you*, and you're a *good* boy. You have done your best to look after me, better than I've done for you."

With her words and the warmth in her eyes, he felt like a grown man, capable and honorable, a good feeling in the hard world in which he found himself.

No, he could not leave his Mum in her time of need.

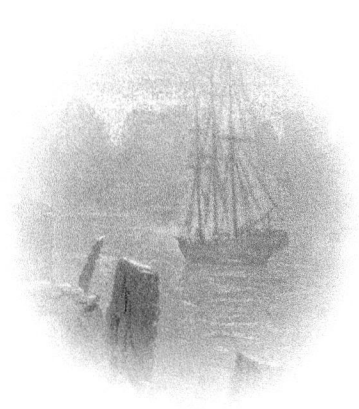

In Dreams or in Sooth

Near dusk, Albert realized he'd lost an entire day that could have been used to salvage from the wherry. He fought with himself, finding his unwillingness to abandon his mother unreasonable. Still, he could think of no falsehood that would give him the time he needed to do the work at the river. Even though making his salvage from the wherry would help Mum too, he couldn't bring himself to admit to her that he'd been lying about how he made his earnings. On his third trip that day from their lodgings to the public pump to fetch a bucket of water, he almost abandoned the errand to go to the river. Darkness had crept up on him, and he decided as he had before that the light necessary to work at the wherry would only bring unwelcome attention to the wreck in the night.

Returning to the dimly-lit interior of their room, he nearly tripped over the heavy porcelain chamber pot resting in the middle of the thin walkway between the bed and the table. The pot, rather full, needed dumping again. Tiny flecks of white swirled about in the colorless waste within.

His mother had returned to bed.

Albert placed his bucket on the open central shelf of the corner hutch, dipped water from it into a cup for Mum, and set the cup on the bedstead. Lifting the brimming chamber pot, he carefully took the vessel out and poured the fluid into the privy vault. He'd already performed the chore six times that day.

Returning to the room, he found Mum inclined in the bed, drinking from the cup he'd filled for her. Much of the liquid spilled down her stained nightshirt. Although constantly thirsty, she'd had no appetite since falling ill. Her retching produced little but a clear liquid.

"I'm hungry, Mum," Albert said, hoping she'd send him out for food. If she did, he'd have the excuse to visit the wherry, perhaps cut a few rushes from elsewhere along the foreshore to throw atop the vessel to help keep it hidden. He could do that in the dark. If he ran the whole way there and back, she might not miss him.

"Bit of toke," Mum said, her words gummy from lack of spittle. She gestured toward the upper cabinet of the hutch where she stored the edibles.

Resentfully—he felt little hunger, despite his protestation—Albert found and ate the crust that remained of a loaf of bread, the last bit of food in their room.

Not long after dark, he began to suffer a severe loosening of the bowels, with a thin, watery discharge. He tried not to think that he would soon find himself in the same condition as his mother. During a lull in the seemingly endless evacuation, he donned his nightshirt, got in the bed on the side next to the wall, and lay down beside Mum.

Albert found a fitful slumber. He tossed and turned through much of the night. During a dream of scavenging the wreck of the wherry, he knew himself to be partly awake. In that half-dream, he found beautiful porcelain, and a shilling amidst the silt near the boat's prow. He seized upon that vision of discovery, reliving it several times in an effort to give substance to the hope it seemed to represent. Each time the discovery was a little different; the porcelain became table silver; the single shilling became two, then the coins became gold

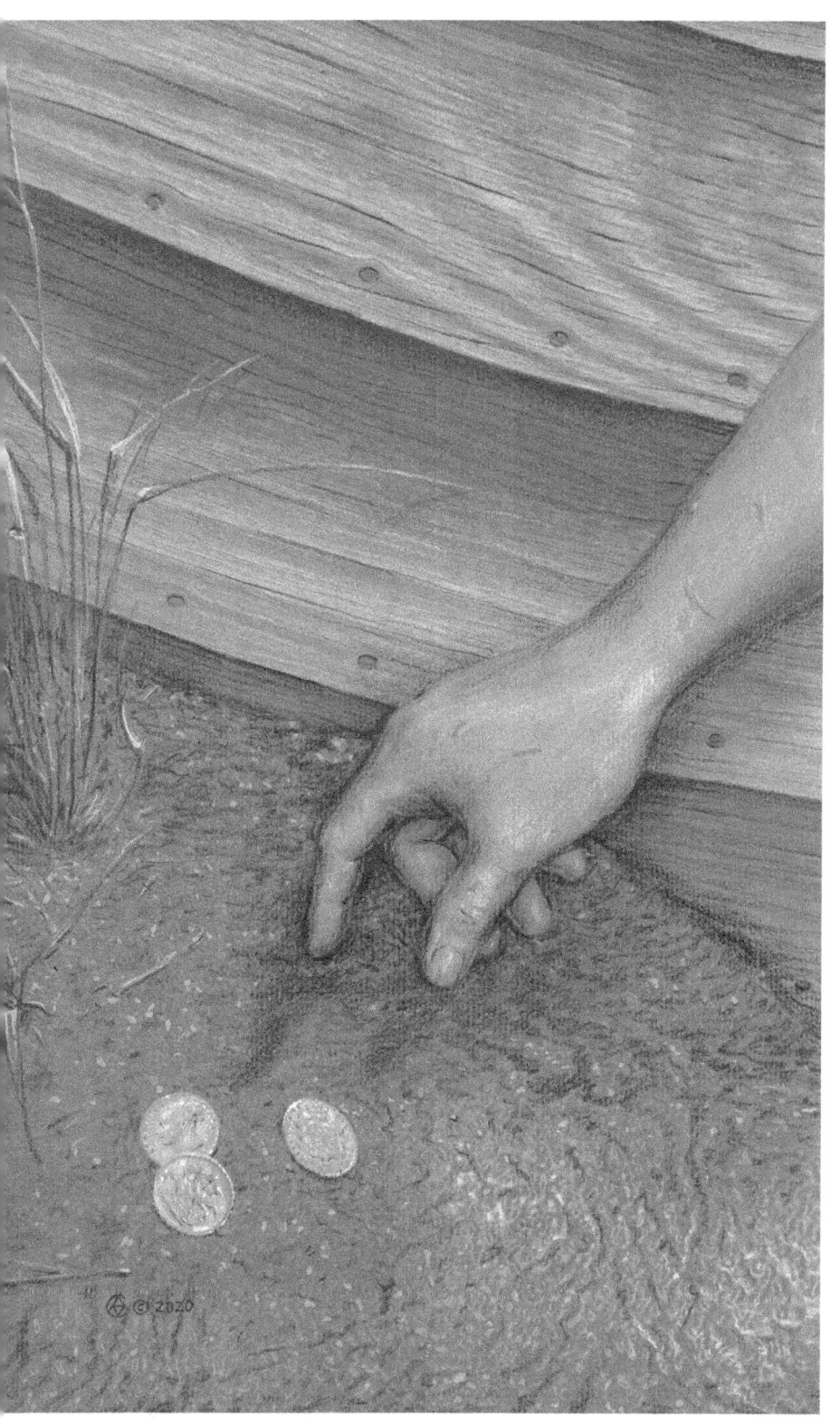

sovereigns.

A rumbling gut and a memory of something Papa had said about gold brought him fully awake for a moment. Albert turned to face the wall as he remembered. His father had been drunk and ranting angrily. "Gold has no worth but what the fancy of men give it. Those in the upper classes, though they have the advantage, they are not truly our betters."

What an odd notion, Albert had thought at the time. Must be the drink—*everyone knows gold is valuable.*

Returning to his half-dream, he saw George Hardly approaching the wreck. Albert crouched down among the rushes, fearing he might have been seen. He scooped up a handful of mud to throw at Hardly if necessary, and held his breath, watching silently. The older boy seemed unwilling to look directly toward the area of the white lead works drain. He gave it a wide berth and moved on along the curve of the muddy foreshore.

Albert plucked the coins—now three gold sovereigns—out of the silt near the prow of the wherry, placed them in the hidden pocket inside the buttoned waistband of his breeches, and hurried away.

Half awake, he knew the vision to be pure fancy. Still, the sense of hope it gave allowed him to ignore the misery of his situation.

Since his mother no longer made an effort to keep from fouling the bed, Albert also allowed himself to let go his bowels as he lay there. He would help Mum clean the mattress ticking and stuff it with fresh straw later. For a short time, he found deeper slumber.

The Silent Highwayman's Doings

Fully awake at last as morning light entered the sooty window of their lodgings, Albert rocked in the damp, chilly bedclothes, unable to gather the will to rise. Finally, the wetness beneath him and the malodorous night air in the bed drove him to his feet. Although he felt worse than he had the night before—truly wrung out—Albert had to find his strength. With Mum down with illness, providing the daily victuals fell to him.

Again, he thought resentfully of his father.

Even if he were about, he'd be no help. Good riddance.

Mum remained asleep, lying on her back. She slept so peacefully, even her usual soft snoring had ceased. Her lower left leg hung over the edge of the mattress. Albert lifted the stiff gray limb and placed it back in the bed. Her skin felt cold to his touch. Trying not to disturb her for fear that she'd keep him from leaving, he pulled the untidy bed clothes over her, tucking them up around her shoulders and down around her dry feet.

A hollow ache in his gut told him to eat, but they had nothing left. Just as well—he had to make his salvage, sell what he could, hopefully earn enough to buy some meat or fish. He would eat later.

His muscles moving with reluctance, Albert removed his sodden nightshirt and dressed himself for the day. Fluid ran down his legs

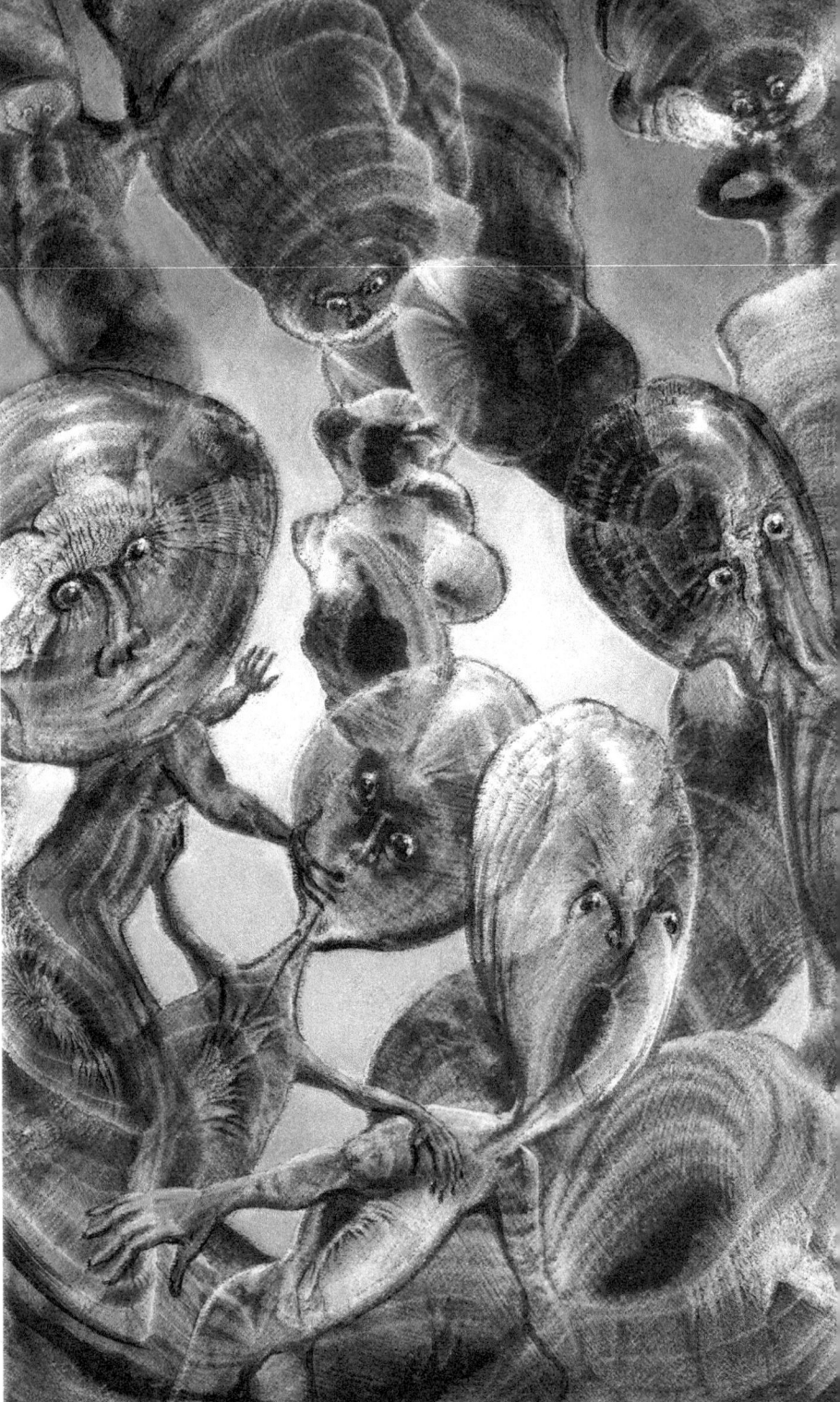

and into his shoes as he opened the door. Thinking of the embarrassment he would experience if anyone saw he'd wet his breeches gave him little pause. He stepped from the lodgings and staggered along Narrow Street, then south on Bridge Road.

The Thames had made him ill again, and he bore the shame of having brought the sickness from the river to Mum as well.

Common wisdom held that illness came from bad smells, those of the river and the night air of privies and countless other places of rot and decay. Some said that wasn't true, that illnesses came instead from creatures in the water so small they couldn't be seen. Albert's few attempts to imagine such beings, were not frightening enough to be believable.

He might have blamed the grundylows, but had somehow decided they were pure make-believe.

No, the sickness is the Silent Highwayman's doings, he thought, trying unsuccessfully to cast aside his feeling of guilt.

A few who saw him gave concerned looks, yet nobody stopped to ask after his welfare. He didn't expect any attention or help. So many children wandered the streets, ragged, ill, neglected, and unwanted. At least *he* had his Mum.

Albert passed the Limehouse Basin, crossed over two locks, took a right into Cuba Street, headed for the West India Docks Pier.

With little distance to go before reaching the path that led down to the water's edge, he heard, "Little boy!"

The voice came from behind him. He twisted his stiff neck around to see George Hardly emerging from between two warehouses about a hundred yards away.

Albert hurried forward, his throat clenching on dryness as he tried to swallow, the pulse in his throat suddenly rapid, his head clearing even as he felt a separation from his body.

"Where are you going?" Hardly shouted. "Stop, or you'll be sorry."

The sound of rapid footsteps came from behind.

Having taken that trek so many times in recent days, Albert was able to move in an unthinking manner, somehow keeping his frantic feet under him. He dreaded the twenty-foot climb down the steep embankment beside the pier almost as much as he feared George Hardly catching up. If he got to the water, he might hide among the stumps of old pilings beneath the pier.

A group of laborers parted to allow Albert to stumble past on the footway. Shortly after, Hardly's rapid steps ended abruptly and with a short outburst, as if bodies had collided.

"You want to take more care," someone said in anger.

"Out of my way," came Hardly's voice.

"He's got a knife!" came another voice.

"Yeah, but it's such a little one," came a third, with a scoffing chuckle.

Albert didn't look back. Where the cobblestones of Cuba Street ran out, he dodged to the left around the iron pier, slowed, and started down the eroded bank seam.

"Let me by," Hardly shouted, then came the sounds of a scuffle and a sharp cry.

Albert tried to take more care with his steps. Some of the loose granite cobbles of the road had tumbled partway down the steep incline and become wedged in the seam long ago, providing footholds. Albert put his weight on one and it gave way. He rolled sideways, hit the rough dirt to his left, and tumbled forward ten feet through the air.

Landing headfirst on the dense sand at the river's edge, he heard a loud crack in his neck and shoulder, and the world around him lost some of its color, everything going gray as he became still.

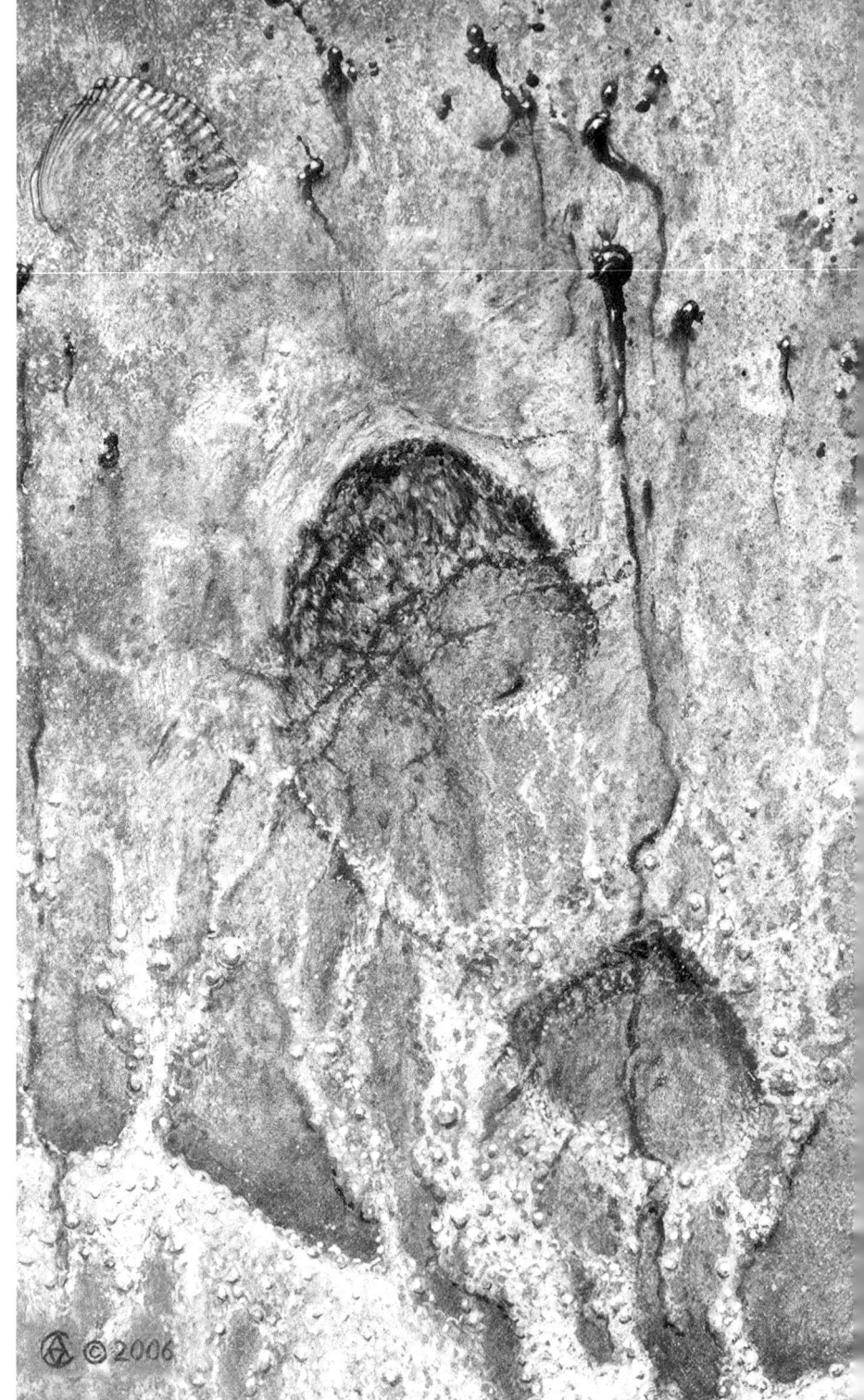

A Time of Remembrance

Surprised that he had not hurt himself, Albert rose awkwardly. His feet, still in his shoes, sank deep into mud. That didn't seem right. But then he remembered that Hardly had been in pursuit. Albert tried to look back the way he'd come, and found he couldn't change the angle of his vision.

His muddied head wouldn't move! His right cheek and ear rested on his shoulder. Everything appeared sideways.

Albert turned his body—the only way to realign his vision—glancing around quickly.

The pier—*gone!*

Something happened…I don't remember…

Had he fallen in the water and been carried downstream?

He kept trying to move his head, looking out for danger.

Nothing there, or, at least, very little. Everything, including the sky, had taken on a similar shade of gray. A near featureless foreshore extended into the dreary distance to either side and behind him.

Why can't I move my head? Have I broken my neck?

He reached up to feel with his hands.

Yes—he felt bones pushing the muscle and skin of his neck outward. Yet he felt no pain.

That fall should have killed me!

He felt fortunate to have survived, and thought of another incident in his life in which luck had safeguarded him. A draft horse had kicked him in the head while Albert reached for a farthing that had got away from him and rolled off the kerb to lie beneath a wagon. The force of the blow had tossed him at least ten feet onto the flagstone footway, but he had walked away with only a gash on his forehead.

Albert would have to take care not to make his neck worse before he could mend up. He might need a surgeon's help.

An odd quiet suggested his hearing had somehow suffered from the fall. Snapping his fingers told him that wasn't so. What had happened to the rumbling hubbub of the city surrounding the river, the sounds of countless feet, hooves, and wheels upon the stones of the roads, the innumerable voices of the inhabitants, the ringing grind and clank of industry, and commerce on land and in the river?

The disorienting sideways view became tolerable in short order. He saw clearly the chill, gray river, its slow current lapping at the colorless mud along the edge. The bank had a different shape from what he'd expect to see near the West India Docks Pier, it's curve more gentle. With the morning sun low in the eastern sky behind the embankment at his back, he should see its light shining upon the buildings across the moving water to the west. Instead, he saw merely dim silhouettes of the landscape; a couple of rocky prominences, a couple of dead trees, and no more. He saw no river traffic.

Yes, taken downstream. Just don't remember.

Albert turned to his right and began walking upstream.

In the distance, he saw a figure, a scavenger perhaps. Abandoning his natural caution, Albert ran toward the figure, but his vision, bouncing with his head on his shoulder, became too disorienting. Slowing, he got a good look. A boy, it seemed, crouched on the foreshore, poking at the mud with a stick. He wore several layers of mud-caked clothing, mostly rags, and some sort of large, cumbersome hat

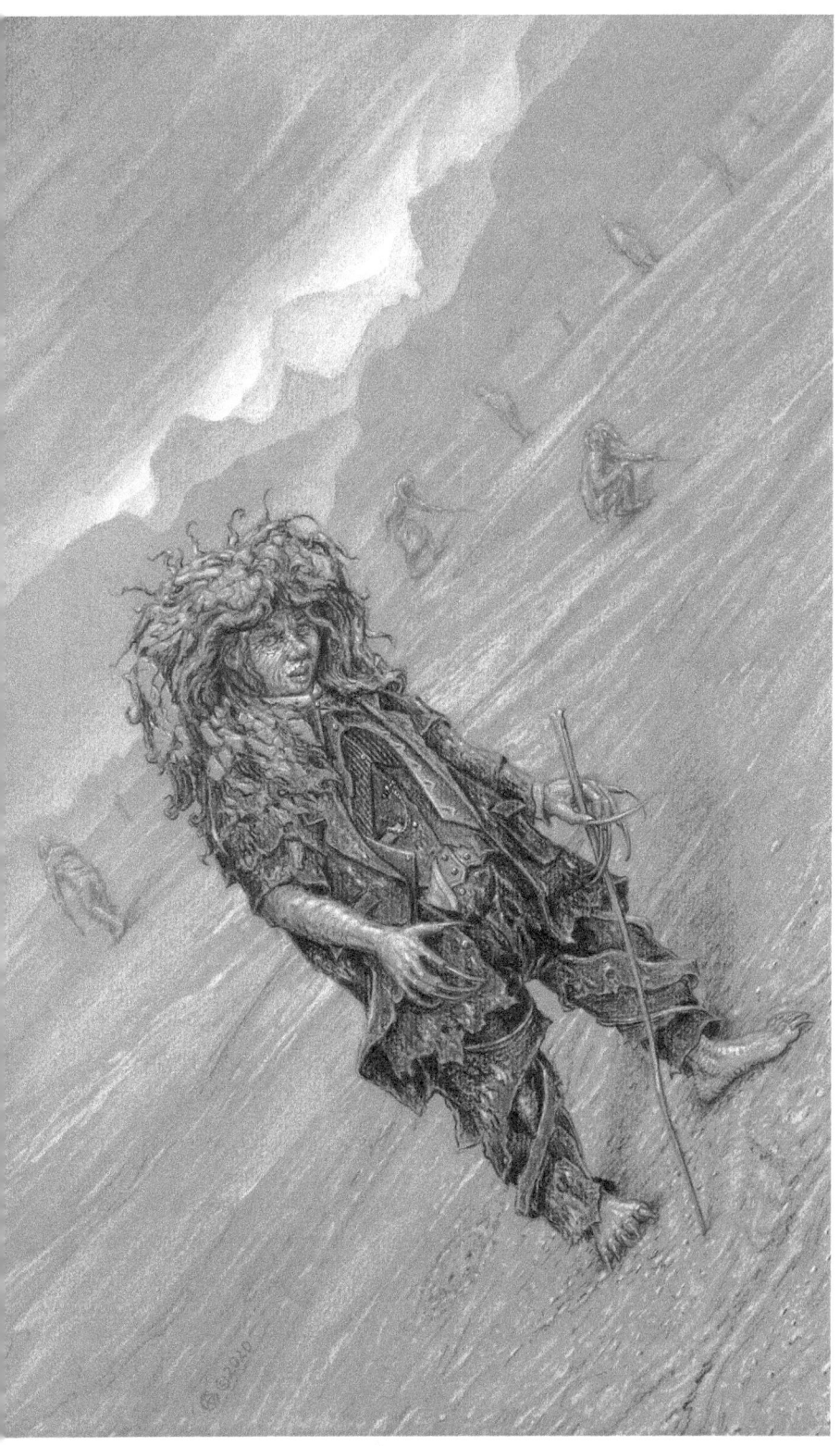

upon his head. No—not a hat, but a mass of filth-clotted, tangled hair, also caked, as if he, too, had fallen head-first in the mud. The figure seemed a growth on the gray landscape. Displaying no curiosity, let alone wariness—something unusual in a scavenger—the child didn't look up as Albert approached.

"Tell me, please," Albert said, "where are we on the river?"

Like an old man, bent and broken with age, the boy rose slowly. For all his filth, he had a gold watch chain fixed to one of his numerous waistcoats, the end disappearing into a pocket, where, presumably, a watch rested. So, indeed a scavenger, and a successful one too.

Finally, he lifted his head.

Albert gasped to see the features beneath the rat's nest of hair. Yes, a child—the rounded shape of the face told that—though wrinkled with untold years of wear on what otherwise had a boyish shape. The lips and nostrils suffered cracks at the edges. The eyes, dull and somehow vacant, held the smallest hint of a great yearning deep inside. Indeed, Albert could see in the silent pleading gaze a curious and inquisitive boy, a poor waif trapped within an ancient, slow-moving body.

Revulsion drove Albert back a few stumbling steps. He felt the tingling of his skin tightening into gooseflesh.

The ancient boy dropped the stick, raised his hands toward Albert. The fingernails were several inches long, curled in upon themselves, some raggedly broken.

Albert turned and ran despite the disorienting effect of his bouncing vision.

The grayness seemed to absorb him. His mind having nothing visual to grab onto, he lost all sense of direction and feared that he might make a circle, running into the boy again. Albert stopped and turned, saw the boy not too far away. He'd picked up his stick, gone back to poking at the mud, and didn't appear to be a threat.

A muffled cry of, "My eye!" seemed to come from the mud beneath his stick.

"My apologies," the boy said in a thin, cracked voice.

Did I awaken or is this still dream?

Albert looked closely at the back of his right hand, saw a smear of soil caught in the tiny hairs, the grit trapped beneath his nails, and a bit of dried grass caught in a sharp split of his thumbnail. He pressed that nail hard into his index finger until he felt pain.

No, not dreaming.

Continuing to back away from the boy, Albert found himself standing in a few inches of foamy river water. The current angle of his head allowed him to see what lay at his feet: A spill of blood oozing across one of his footprints.

A tap on his left shoulder, and he spun around.

George Hardly!

Albert stumbled back and fell on his arse in the water, scrambled backwards on all fours out of the river to get away. Hardly followed.

Albert could see only the boy's torn breeches and feet, the shoe missing from the left foot. He turned onto his side to see more of him.

Hardly held his hands out to his sides. His scarred face, wide eyes, and trembling lips had a pleading look.

Even so, Albert covered his head with his arms for protection, drew his knees to his chest.

"I mean no harm," Hardly said, his voice tremulous.

Albert peeked up at him from between fingers. The older boy appeared on the verge of tears. Hardly reached out a hand. Though reluctant, Albert finally took it and stood with assistance. The two boys looked at one another.

Hardly's shirt was bloodied and had a hole in it on the left side of his chest. "He had a bigger knife," he said with a grimace. "I fell down the bank, got lost. I recognize you, but nothing else." He grimaced again. "What happened to your head?"

"I fell on it." Albert backed away. "Leave me be."

"I know… I-I harmed you," Hardly said. "I don't expect you'll forgive, but I need to find my brothers. This wants help." He gestured toward the hole in his chest, looking fearful. "Your head wants help too."

Albert continued shuffling backwards. Hardly kept up, walking slowly.

"Stay away," Albert said, and the other boy slowed, following from a distance.

He saw the figure of a young girl ahead, another filthy waif in rags, not quite so bent with age as the ancient boy he'd seen earlier. She'd lost most of her right arm. A withered nub hung out of her gray, rotting shift. Moving toward the girl, Albert watched her poke at something in the mud with a stick held in her remaining hand. "Just a rock," she said, presumably to herself. She spoke slowly, as if the effort was practiced, not natural. "No life, no memories."

He stopped to speak to her. Hardly became still about fifty feet away.

"Can you tell me where I am?" Albert asked.

She looked him in the eye. Although appearing sad and withdrawn, her gaze didn't frighten. She had crow's feet at the corners of her eyes and creases around her mouth, much like those of Albert's mother. Her skin had the liver spots of someone much older still.

"Sticks," she said, simply.

He looked at the stick in her hand.

"What did she say?" Hardly asked.

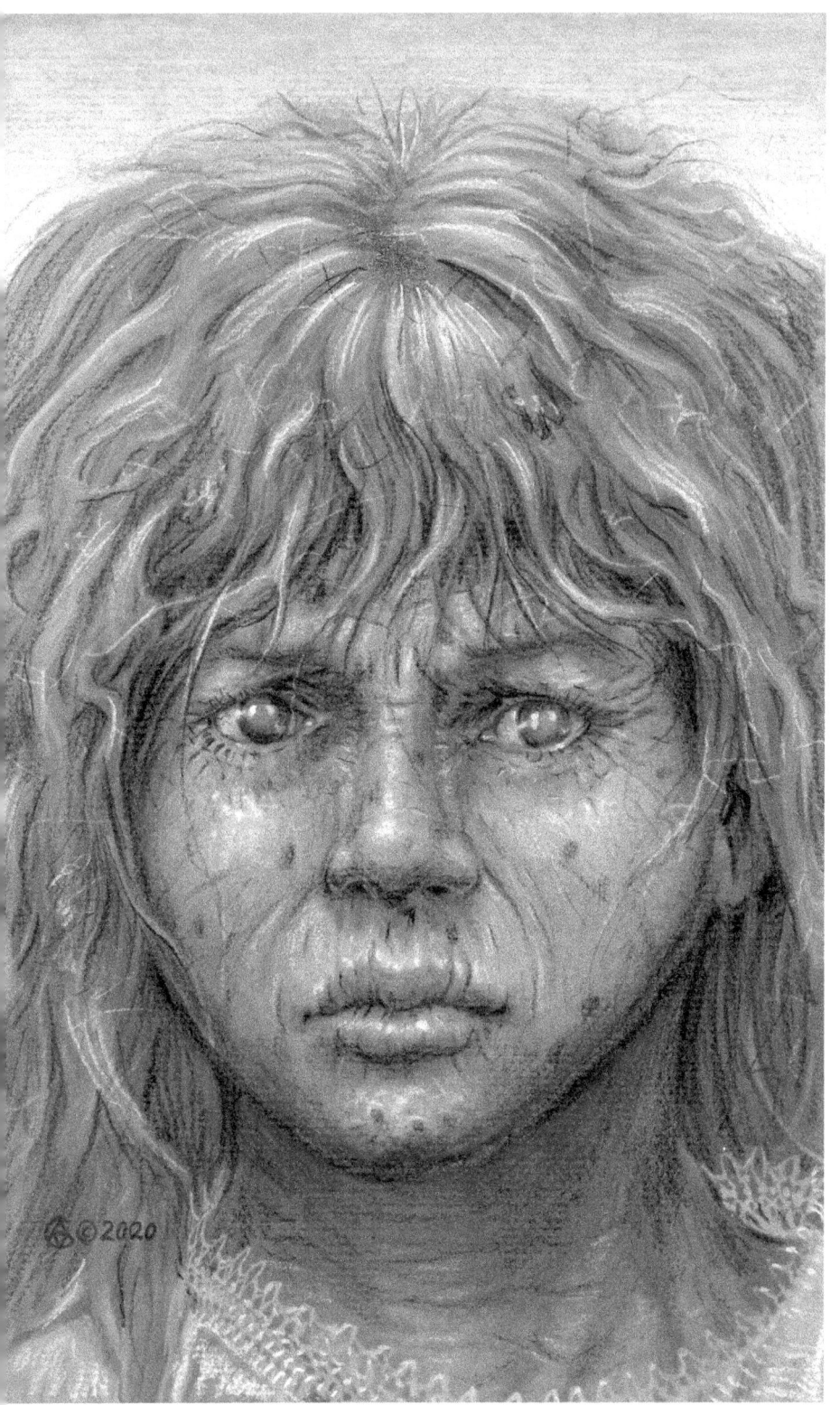

Albert waved the older boy's words away. "Do you live hereabouts?" he asked the girl.

Her eyes widened briefly at the word, "live." The crow's feet disappeared. For a moment, she looked like any little girl. She seemed to search his face for meaning.

Albert became uncomfortable, trapped within her gaze.

Then a brief look of fright fixed her features. The crow's feet returned. "The woolen mill, that's where I…" Her voice trailed off for a moment. "The machine was so thirsty, never got enough of the oil, never satisfied. Had a hunger too…" She left the stick upright in the mud and rubbed the nub of her right arm. "…and a mean bite."

Finally the girl frowned and her gaze shifted. She shrugged, and took up her stick. "You've only just come, you and your friend," she said, turning away and poking the mud. "You know nothing."

Hardly had approached. "Do you live here?" he asked the girl.

"No live," she said, "no die. No coins. One hundred years before I can go without paying the fare. Maybe tomorrow—don't know how long I've been here. Not as long as he has done." She gestured toward the boy Albert had first approached, now a mere thirty yards away.

The air having cleared slightly, Albert saw several other children wandering the river's edge in the hazy distance. Their movements slow and unnatural for children, he assumed they all suffered the same condition, whatever that was.

"Which way to Limehouse?" Hardly said. He grabbed the girl by the shoulders. The nub of her right arm broke off in his grip. He threw it to the ground as if it had stung him, and looked at the girl, his mouth gaping in horror. She made no complaint, nor any expression of pain or surprise.

Hardly's astonishment emerged as a great whooping sound. Then he was in a rapid stumble to get away. He disappeared into the grayness.

Albert, transfixed by the drama, stood dumbly wondering how he might help the girl. "Are you…?" he began.

The girl looked briefly at the nub of her arm on the foreshore before turning away toward the river.

Is she so ill she cannot feel? Has he made them all sick?

Albert hadn't wanted to believe Thomas's tale of the Silent Highwayman, but now he easily accepted that the skeletal phantom existed.

He's done this, and now…

"Luck is with you," the girl said, pointing out over the water. "He comes for you."

Albert saw a small boat, much like his wherry. From its stem, a green lantern swung, sending out a sickly light that infected nearby mists. A gaunt cloaked figure stood at the tiller. The water appeared unusually troubled beneath the boat.

A panic in Albert's chest shifted to his throat, raising his head upright, and he ran, the muddy foreshore sucking on his every step. He made it to firmer ground, picked up speed, only to stumble on something in his path. Falling, he rolled and lifted himself quickly to his feet.

Albert saw what had tripped him—Papa's winning smile, half-submerged in the muck. Mud had oozed into the open mouth, slid in a smear across the uneven teeth, but Albert would recognize that grin anywhere.

He reached—he had to help if his father were somehow trapped alive under the mud.

Upon touching his father's lips, he knew his mother's feelings for the man, their history together.

She'd become pregnant while unwed. Her family, too poor to feed another hungry child, turned her out in the street. Mum had

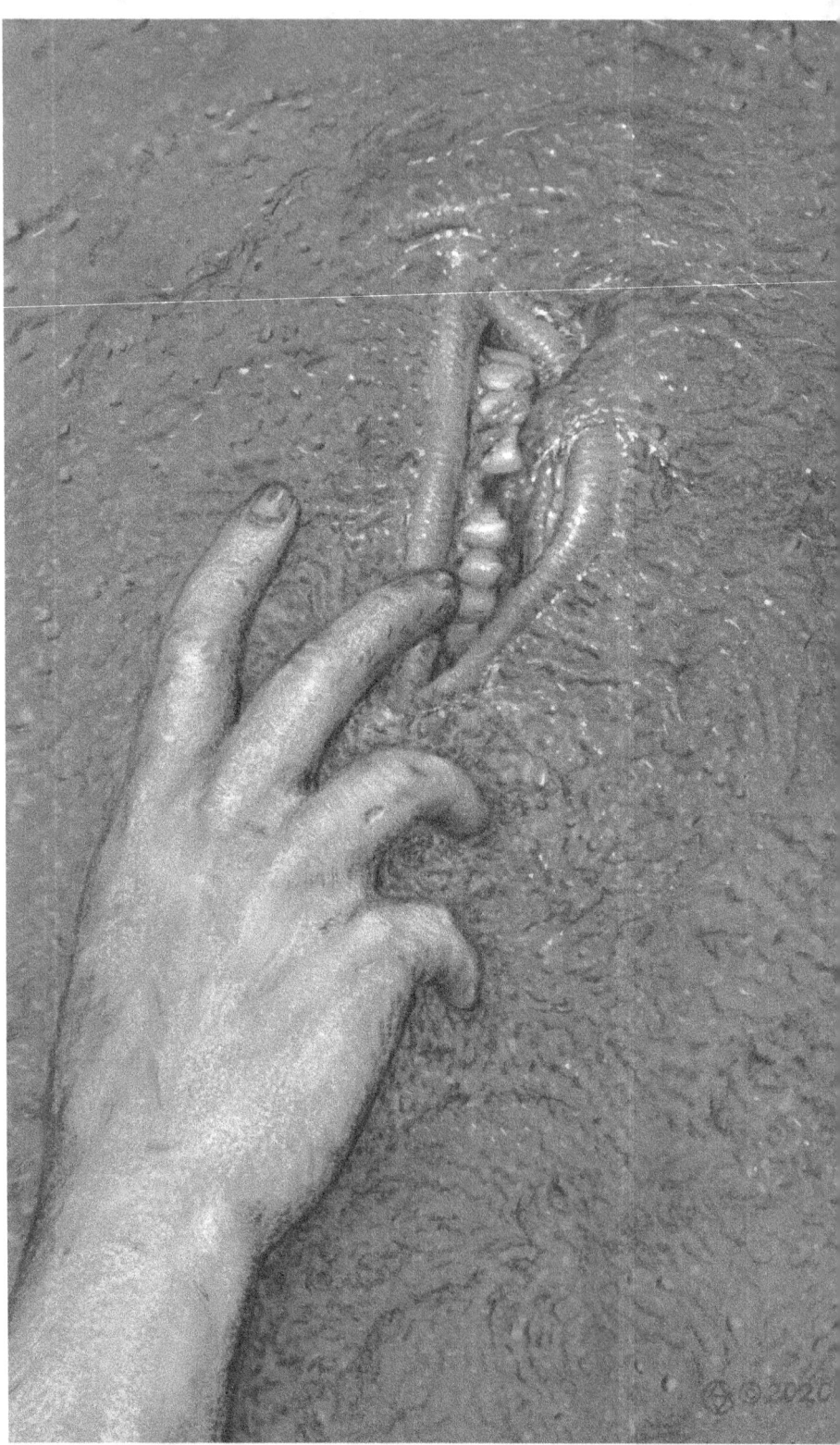

a meager income working as a cardroomer at a fearnought mill. She could barely afford lodgings of her own. Soon to be a mother needing an income more than ever, she'd fallen under the thumb of the mill's overlooker, a cruel man named Ganloff.

Papa competed for fares at the Kidney Stairs in Limehouse, very near the fearnought mill. At midday, he'd take a break, purchase food from a street vendor, and have a stroll while eating. On one of those walks, he found Mum in the alley that ran beside the fearnought mill, hiding behind a stack of crates, her hands covering her face.

"Come, share my bread and cheese," he'd said. "You appear to be eating for two, though you're very thin."

He coaxed her out of her hiding place, took care to gain her trust, and asked for her story.

"I'm too ashamed to tell it," she said, her red-rimmed eyes downcast.

Papa gave her a gentle smile, said, "There's nothing that unburdens one so much as telling the worst to a willing stranger. Should you trust me, whatever it is, I shan't think the less of you for it."

She did not confide in him on that day.

With his smile and good humor, he lifted her heart and she laughed many times during their first meal together. They met in the alley at midday many times over the following month.

One day, she placed her hands on her swollen belly and said, "When the father found out I were knapped, he left me and went to sea. Mr. Ganloff found out, said should I want to keep my position, I'd please him and his three brothers. All are scurfs here at the mill. No one disobeys them. Some of the women they command are pimped on the street. Once the baby comes, that's where they'll send me."

Papa courted Mum briefly. Already friends, true affection drew them even closer. He asked for Mum's hand. She quit the mill and married him before young Albert was born. Mum had asked Albert Gladwick senior if she could give his name to her boy.

He loved me—raised me as his own.

He saved Mum from the street! No wonder she'd forgive him anything.

Along with the revelations of Mum's past came the understanding that she had died in the night. Passing on, she'd dropped his father's smile on the foreshore. Though the flesh felt real, somehow Albert knew the grin to be mere memory.

Distracted by the experience, consumed by his feelings of loss, Albert had forgot briefly about the one approaching in the boat. Sudden realization of the need to flee forced a gulping breath that brought back the panic.

He wiped away his tears, looked out over the water, and saw that the Silent Highwayman had drawn closer, not a hundred yards away.

Albert got up and ran again. Deeper mud confounded his steps and sucked away his energy. Still, he plodded on, moving away from the water. Periodically looking back, he saw that the river remained beside him—he could not put distance between himself and the water, nor between himself and the one in the boat.

So concerned with what lay behind him, not watching his step, he tripped on another object in the mud. His foot had hooked onto something that he now dragged behind him. Turning, he saw he'd pulled what looked like a toy steamship out of the mud. The wet, clay-like soil flowed away from the thing, revealing a motionless burst of fire from a cannon, and equally still black coal smoke above the ship's funnel. About the size of the bucket in which he'd carried water the day before, the small vessel, with its intricate rigging and perfectly formed, unmoving crew on deck, appeared as vividly complex as any

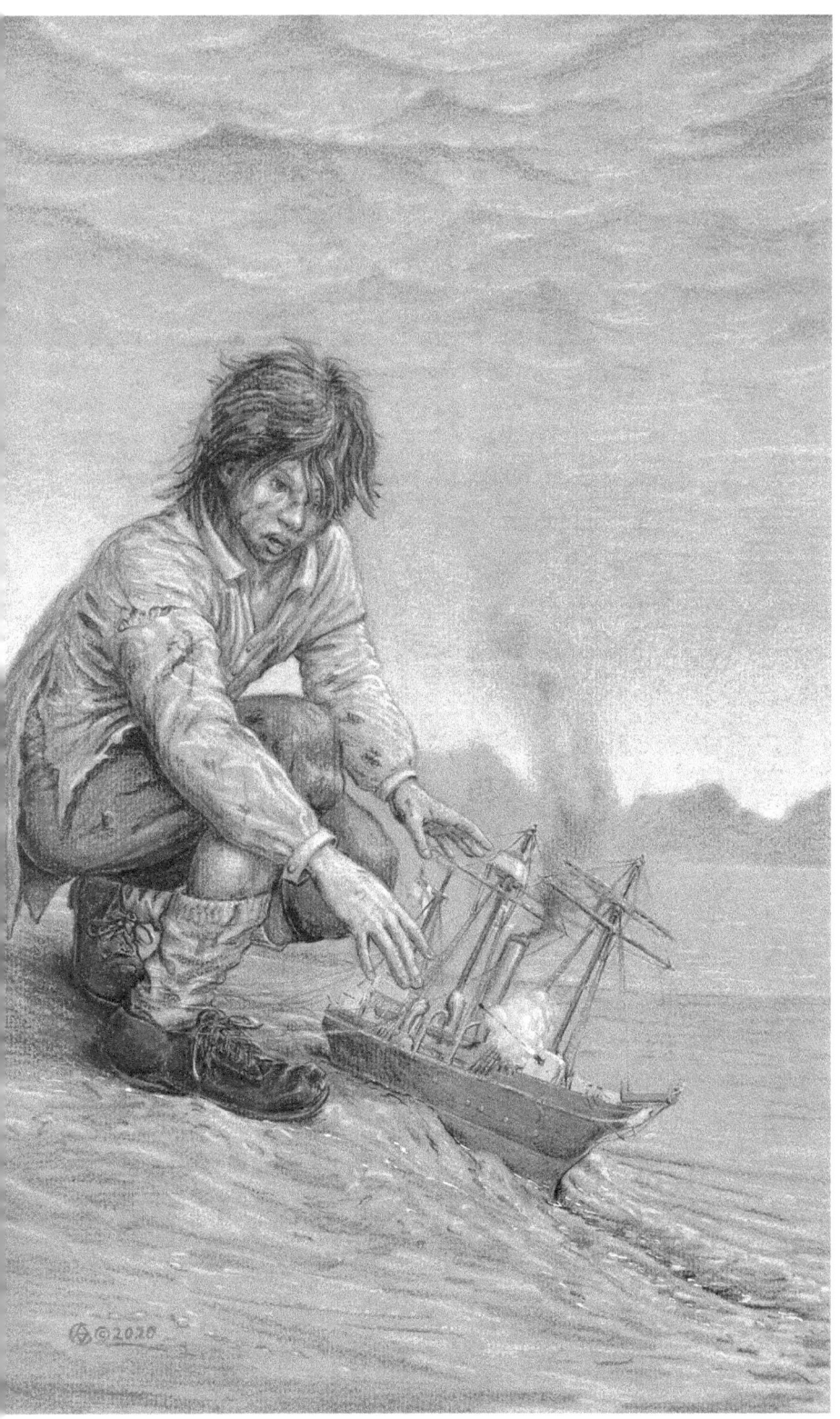

ship he'd ever seen. Its tiny signal flags, though motionless, lifted on an unfelt breeze. Even the smell of it, the coal smoke and a familiar fermentation of aging in the sea, mixed with what he believed to be the odor of spent smokeless powder, confirmed that *it was no toy.*

Albert reached to touch an explosive shell, suspended just ahead of the still and silent flash at a cannon muzzle.

Instantly, he knew his father's horror at finding the dead and dying in Alexandria following the British fleet's three-day-long bombardment of the city. Papa had been among the sailors sent from the fleet to fight alongside the British Expeditionary Force in the battle of Kafr El Dawwar. He'd been wounded and suffered the amputation of his leg, then was left in the heat of a dust and fly ridden field hospital to recover with little to help relieve his pain. Albert knew the sights of mutilation, the sounds of agony, the stench of blood that had become lodged in Papa's mind from his time in the Anglo-Egyptian War.

Having refused to fire upon young boys conscripted by the Egyptian forces to fight against the British, Papa had been the subject of a court-martial. With consideration for the loss of his limb, his sentence was merely the loss of his pension. Much worse, he'd lost his pride.

Compassion for Albert Gladwick senior welled up in young Albert's heart. Regretting his harsh judgement of the man, he knew again his love for his father.

The ship was a memory of the one Papa had served aboard during the war. He had dropped the small vessel on the muddy foreshore when he'd passed on.

Yes, both his parents had passed away. But away where—where had Papa and Mum gone?

The girl's voice, very close, startled Albert, and he swung around to face her. She had followed, come up from behind, and crouched down beside him in the mud.

"You found a memory," she said, a small delight in her voice, a shade of it in her eyes. "If you want to keep it, you'll have to carry it with you. Looks like a weighty one. May I touch it?"

Albert nodded uncertainly. She reached for one of the tiny ship's flags, and closed her eyes. Her features moved subtly with emotion. Moisture appeared among her dry lashes.

"Alice," she said, as if remembering. "That was my name. Born 1832. I shan't have thought of that without touching the soldier's memory." Her voice had gained more life.

Was her name? Questions arose that Albert found too frightening to ask. *No, she's daft or touched.*

"Who are they?" he asked uneasily, gesturing toward the waifs

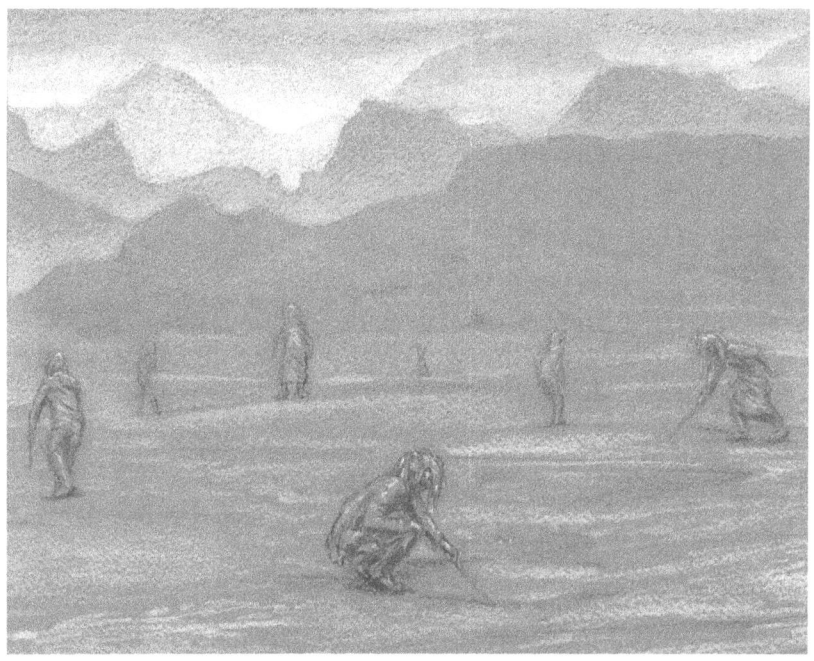

wandering the foreshore in the distance.

"We are orphans and paupers' children, mostly. Paupers who arrive grown have little hope if they are here for long. With time, the heaviness of their hearts weighs them down. They sink deep into the mud and are lost until their time of remembrance is done."

Albert looked down at the mud. As he'd done when finding his father's smile, he pictured the horror of an adult buried beneath him. "How many?" he asked.

"Some arrive each day. Those of us unable to pay to cross over must wait one hundred years."

With his gasp of astonishment, Alice placed her remaining hand, a reassuring one, upon Albert's arm. "You'll not suffer as we do," she said with a touch of envy. Wiping away her gathering tears, she turned toward the water and gestured. "He's here for you."

The cloaked figure in the boat had landed a few yards away.

Albert recoiled, leaning into the small ship's rigging.

The figure made no move toward him, simply held out a hand in greeting, or perhaps to help Albert board the small boat. Silent, yes, but not a highwayman. Albert saw no menace in the pale face beneath the heavy hood.

"There's nothing to fear," Alice said.

She's trapped here, yet she has it in her heart to comfort me?

"You have someone waiting on the other side," she said, not quite asking. "He wouldn't have come if you couldn't pay the fare."

The ferryman, as Papa said! Albert laughed at himself, and the fear Thomas Conway had given him of the Silent Highwayman. *He is not here to rob health, but to carry people across.*

Did he take Papa and Mum? If so, they must have somehow paid the fare.

He saw that the landscape across the river had taken on more color. The sky above reflected something like flowing cloth made of light, so much like the glimpse of the northern lights he and Papa had got from the church tower.

Albert got to his feet. "Perhaps I *do* have someone waiting, but I haven't any chink."

"A coin of any sort will do," Alice said, "even a farthing."

Albert searched. His hip pockets held nothing but gullyfluff.

Frustrated, he looked past Alice, saw George Hardly about twenty yards away. He'd come up quietly, possibly listening.

"Perhaps the ferryman is here for *him*," Albert said. His heart sank at the thought.

Alice turned to look at Hardly. "Oh, yes, I'd forgot," she said. "He awaits payment. Do you have coin, boy?"

Hardly approached cautiously. "No," he said. "To cross the river?"

"Yes," Albert said.

"They put pennies on my grandfather's eyes, someone said to pay…" the older boy began, fear growing in his eyes. "Are we…? Did I…?"

No, Albert thought, *don't say the words. I cannot face it if I hear the words.*

Thankfully, Hardly didn't finish. He shook as if he might shed his troubling thoughts.

"There must be something," Alice said. "He would not have come. I were with a girl when she found a memory of a coin. She let me touch it. The coin was the first earned by a man who became rich, a memory of how he'd built his fortune from humble beginnings. He'd dropped it on the foreshore as he boarded the boat. The ferryman came for the girl after she found it."

"Sir," Hardly said, turning to the one in the boat. "Would you take me to Limehouse? I've suffered grievous harm, and must get home."

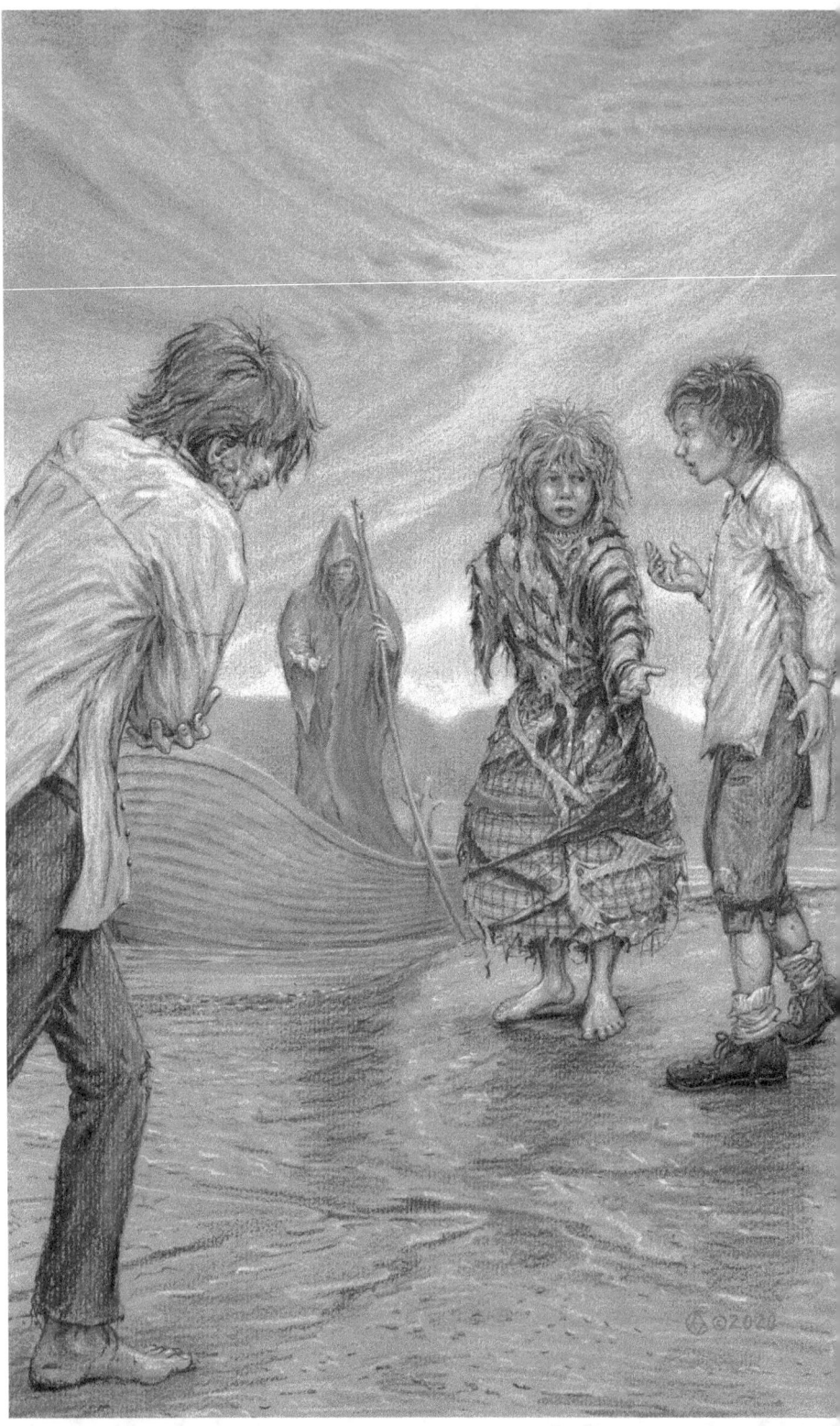

The stoney figure remained stock-still, his hand held out.

Albert turned back to Alice. "Mere remembrance brought forth coin?"

"Yes," she said. "The rich man's coin were like the soldier's ship, a memory."

The mudlark in Albert still sorted between things that should be taken up because they had worth and those to be ignored as worthless. He had been taught that fancies, hopes, and dreams had less value than what might be found in sooth. Yet, considering all that had happened that day, the boundary between actual experience and what occurred within his mind's eye had become mirky. He wasn't at all certain he'd awakened from his dream of the night before.

In that dream he'd found gold sovereigns at the wreck of the wherry. He'd placed the coins in the hidden pocket of his breeches.

"Gold has no worth but what the fancy of men give it," his father had once said.

Against all reason, Albert ran his hand along the waistband of his breeches, trying to make it look like he merely pulled them up in case he was wrong.

He felt cold metal disks through the fabric.

How? I didn't wear my breeches to bed! The foolishness of the thought nearly brought on a laugh, but he held it back.

Three coins, more than I need.

He might give one to Alice. She was deserving. But Hardly?

Albert considered the lesson he'd learned from dealing with Turvey, the one about hardening his heart.

If Hardly sees the gold, will he try to rob me? I could board the boat, leave them both behind. I might need the chink where I'm going.

Albert withdrew the coins, keeping them palmed and hidden. He looked warily at the older boy.

A scared child, George Hardly stood with a forlorn look, holding the hole in his chest with his right hand. He wasn't frightening anymore.

No, a hard heart will get me nothing but the same from others.

Albert stepped up to him and held out a gold sovereign.

Hardly's scarred features twisted grotesquely, but not toward the cruelty they had so often displayed. His brows bunched upward, and his chin quaked. A tear slid from his left eye, as he said, "Thank you."

Albert offered Alice a coin. Looking at the gold in his hand, glinting warmly in the gloom, she stood taller. Color returned to her face. Alice's delighted features became youthful.

"He did not come for you alone!" she said with a giggle.

Boarding the boat, she dropped a dented oil can Albert had not seen in her possession. She seemed unaware that she'd done so.

Similarly, Hardly left behind a blood-stained leather strap.

Stepping into the boat, and paying his fare, Albert wondered briefly what he might have dropped. He didn't turn to look back.

Mere recollection of dream-stuff from the hope of his greatest find—the clinker-built wherry washed up on the foreshore of the Isle of Dogs—the gold had the worth Albert's fancy gave it, enough to pay the fare for all three.

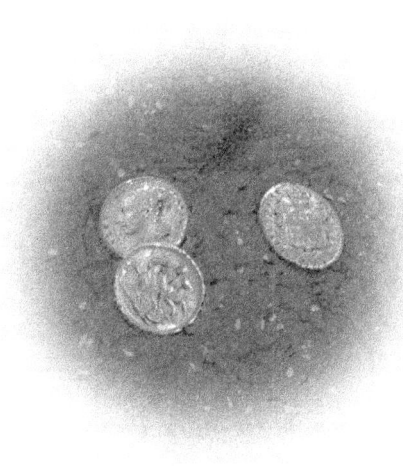

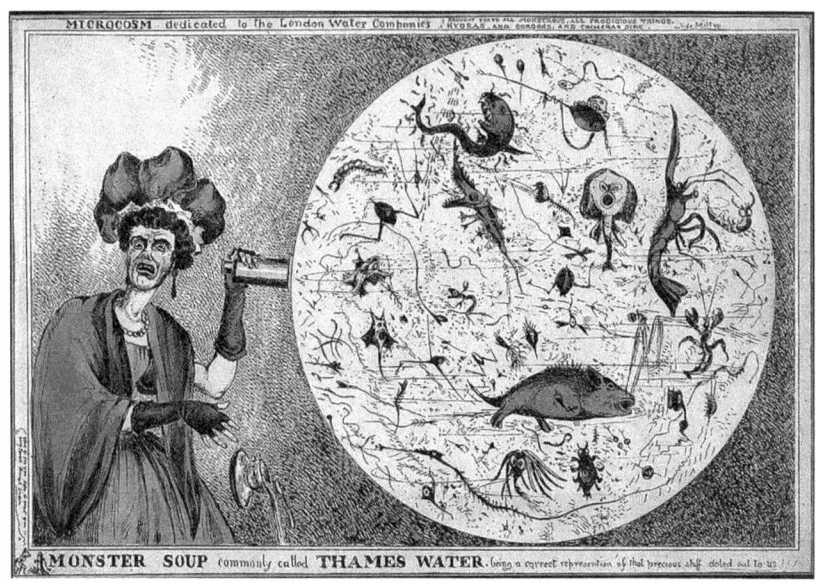

"Monster Soup commonly called Thames Water; being a correct Representation of that Precious Stuff Doled out to Us" Coloured etching by W. Heath, 1828.

Waterborne Illness and The Great Stink

In a time before planes, trains, and automobiles, many cities grew up along rivers because the waterways provided a major means of transportation for both commerce and the public. Rivers were also a dubiously convenient way to rid a city of its waste. During the nineteenth century, London's River Thames was part of the city's failed sewer system, carrying much that was undesirable out of the city: Industrial waste, human and animal waste, dead animals, and not infrequently human corpses. Increasingly overburden with the task as the century progressed, the river was a growing health threat. The waterways that fed the Thames were also known to carry raw sewage.

The majority of Londoners drew their water from public pumps on the streets that were supplied to the city commercially from what the public presumed were potable sources; river water from above the city or from Thames tributaries. As the city and surroundings became what we'd call today a giant sprawl, the amount of raw sewage entering the water system, primarily from human beings and horses, compromised those sources, and periodically caused outbreaks of cholera, dysentery, typhoid, and other diseases.

As people suffered, philanthropists, politicians, journalists joined the public in a fight for a better sewer system. The fight went on for decades as Parliament resisted spending the funds needed for the endeavor. Cartoons give us a glimpse of the public sentiment as expressed through journalism of the time.

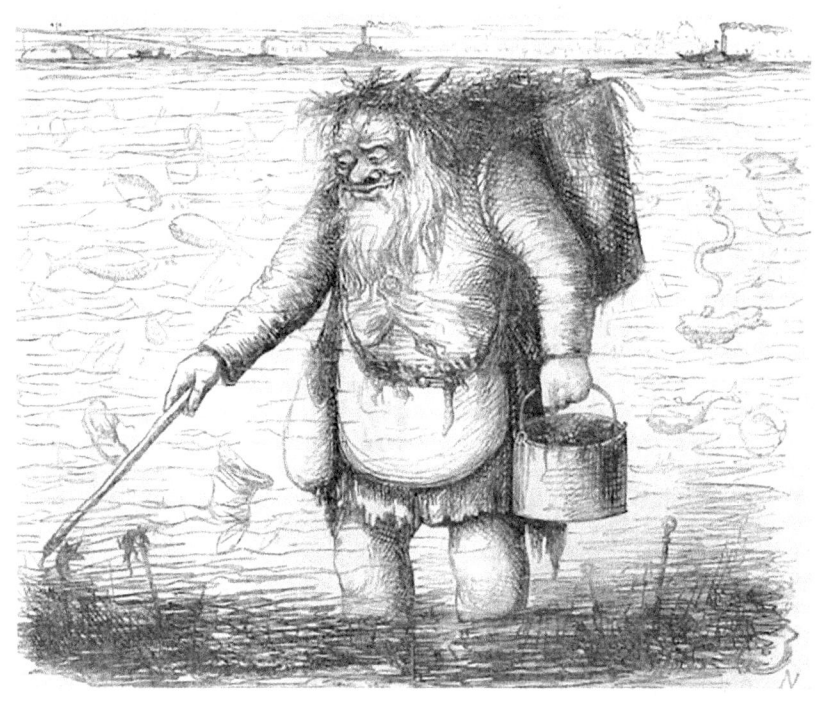

"Dirty Father Thames"
Cartoon and poem from Punch *Magazine October, 1848*

Filthy river, filthy river,
Foul from London to the Nore,
What art thou but one vast gutter,
One tremendous common shore?

All beside thy sludgy waters,
All beside thy reeking ooze,
Christian folks inhale mephitis,
Which thy bubbly bosom brews.

All her foul abominations
Into thee the City throws;
These pollutions, ever churning,
To and fro thy current flows.

And from thee is brewed our porter -
Thee, thou gully, puddle, sink!
Thou, vile cesspool, art the liquor
Whence is made the beer we drink!

Thou too hast a conservator,
He who fills the civic chair;
Well does he conserve thee, truly,
Does he not, my good Lord Mayor?

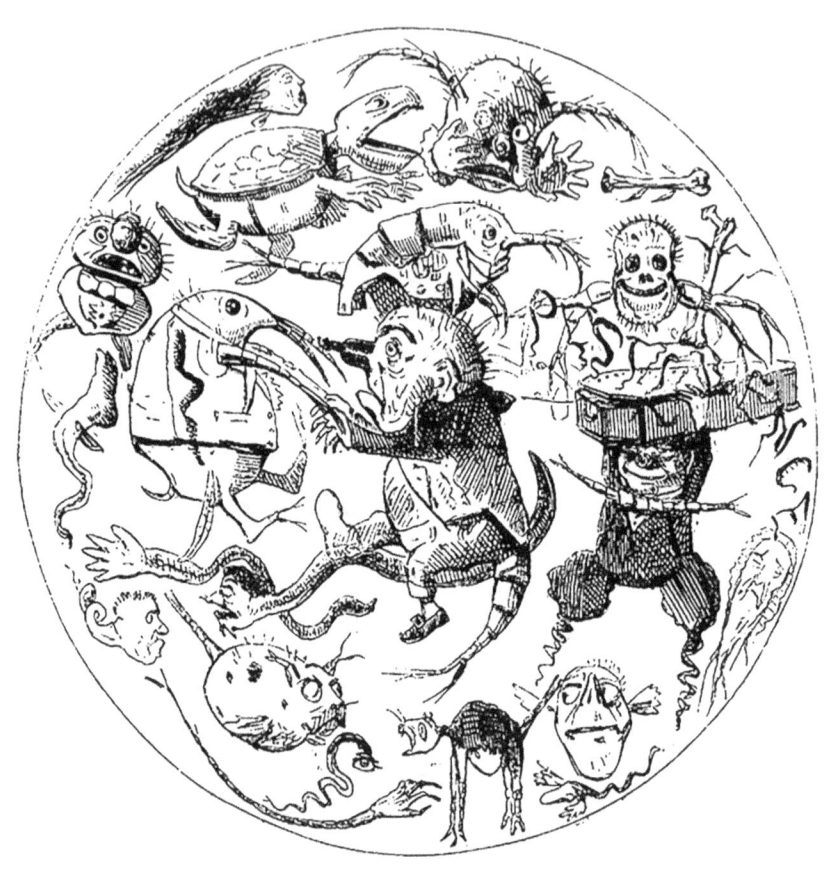

"The Wonders of a London Water Drop"
Punch *magazine May, 1850*

In 1854, physician, John Snow, pinpointed the source of a cholera epidemic as the water supplied from a public pump in Broad Street, Soho. He'd been a proponent of the theory of waterborne transmission of illness over the miasma theory for some time. Demonstrating his scientific method for making the determination, he persuaded the authorities to remove the handle from the pump in question. The epidemic ceased shortly thereafter.

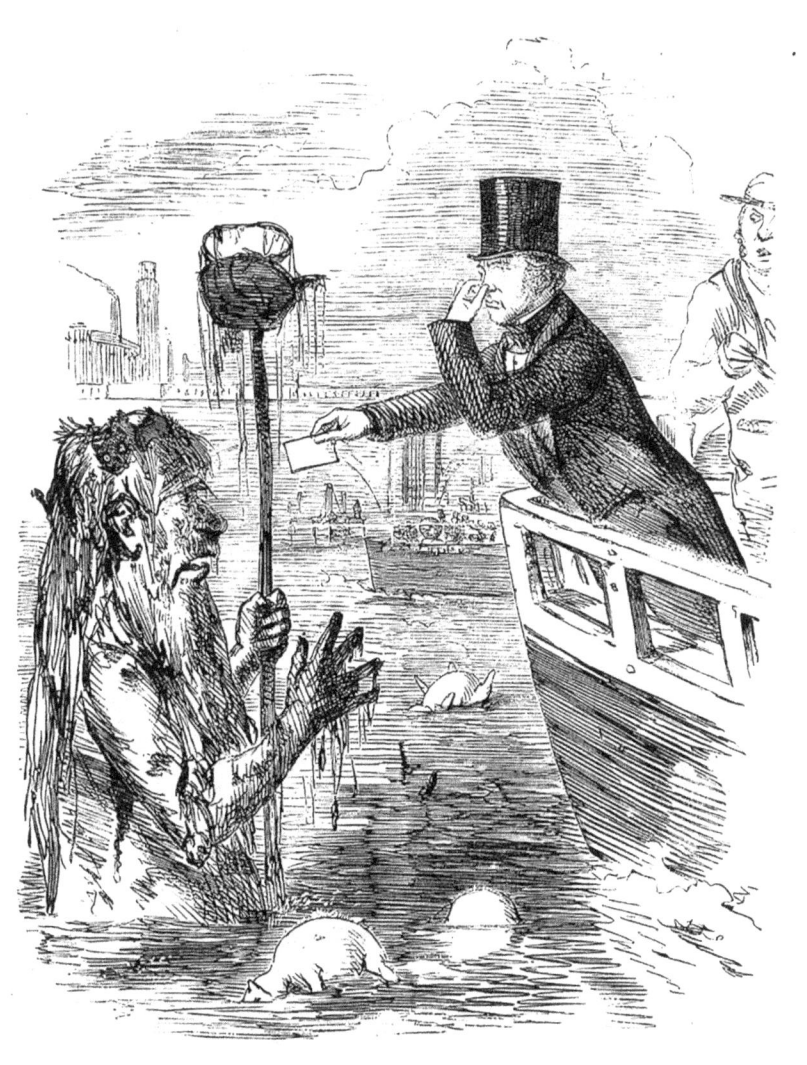

"Faraday giving his card to Father Thames;
And we hope the Dirty Fellow will consult the learned Professor"
Cartoon from Punch Magazine July, 1855

Scientist, Michael Faraday, performed tests at the river in 1855, then warned the public about the threat the water posed.

London's Metropolitan Board of works was established in 1856, intended to unify public works over the whole city.

In 1857 the government tried to reduce the reek coming off the river by dumping chloride of lime and carbolic acid into the water.

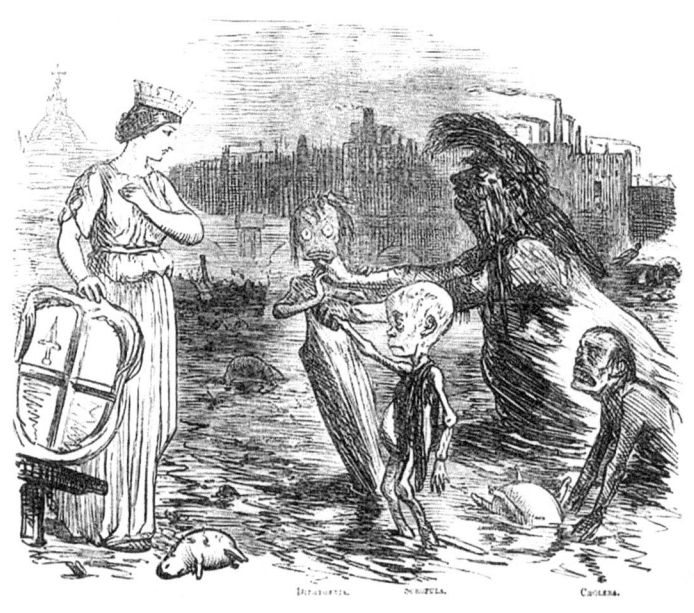

"*Father Thames Introducing His Offspring
to the Fair City of London*"
(A Design for a Fresco in the New Houses of Parliament.)
Engraving by John Leech
Punch *magazine July, 1858*

[The names beneath the "offspring" are Diphtheria, Scrofula, and Cholera]

During The Great Stink in the summer of 1858, the River Thames smelled so bad that Parliament closed for several weeks, and a plan to move the legislative body upstream was considered and rejected. The curtains in Parliament were treated with lime to help reduce the smell.

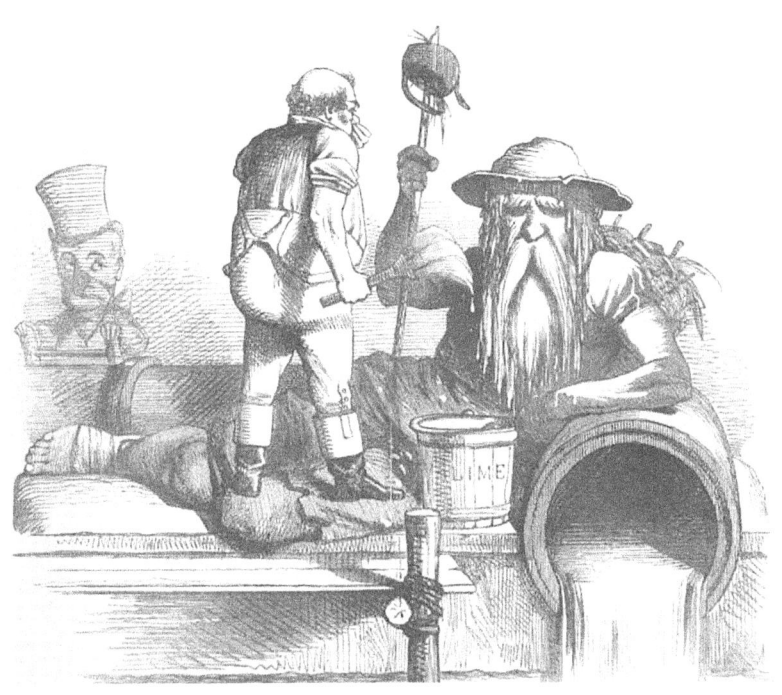

"*How Dirty Old Father Thames was Whitewashed*"
Punch *magazine July, 1858*

[Commentary on the use of lime to cover up the problem]

1866 saw most of London connected to a network of sewers designed by Joseph Bazalgette, one that intercepted city sewage and sent it to a water treatment works. The Thames became much cleaner, and the Silent Highwayman became just another part of history.

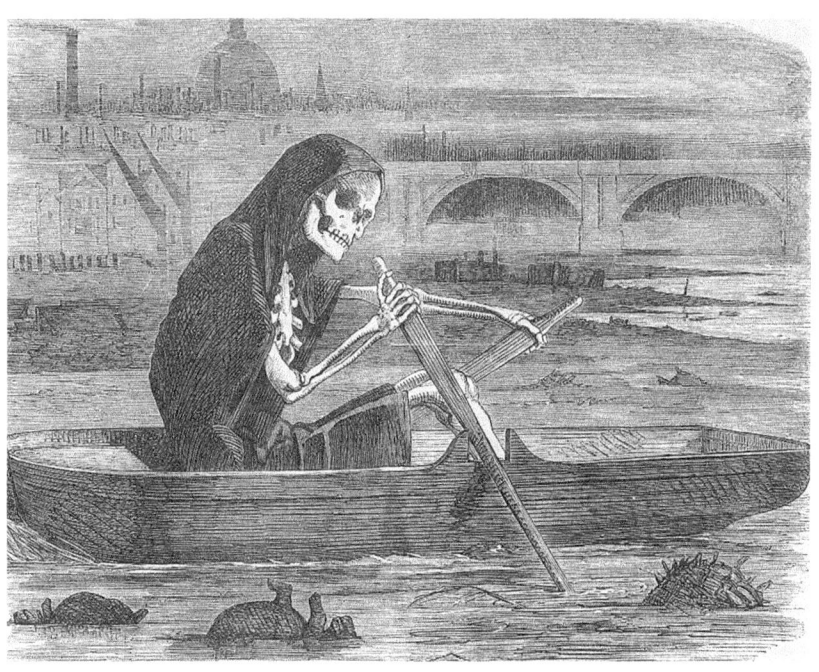

"The Silent Highwayman, Your Money or Your Life"
Punch *magazine July, 1858*

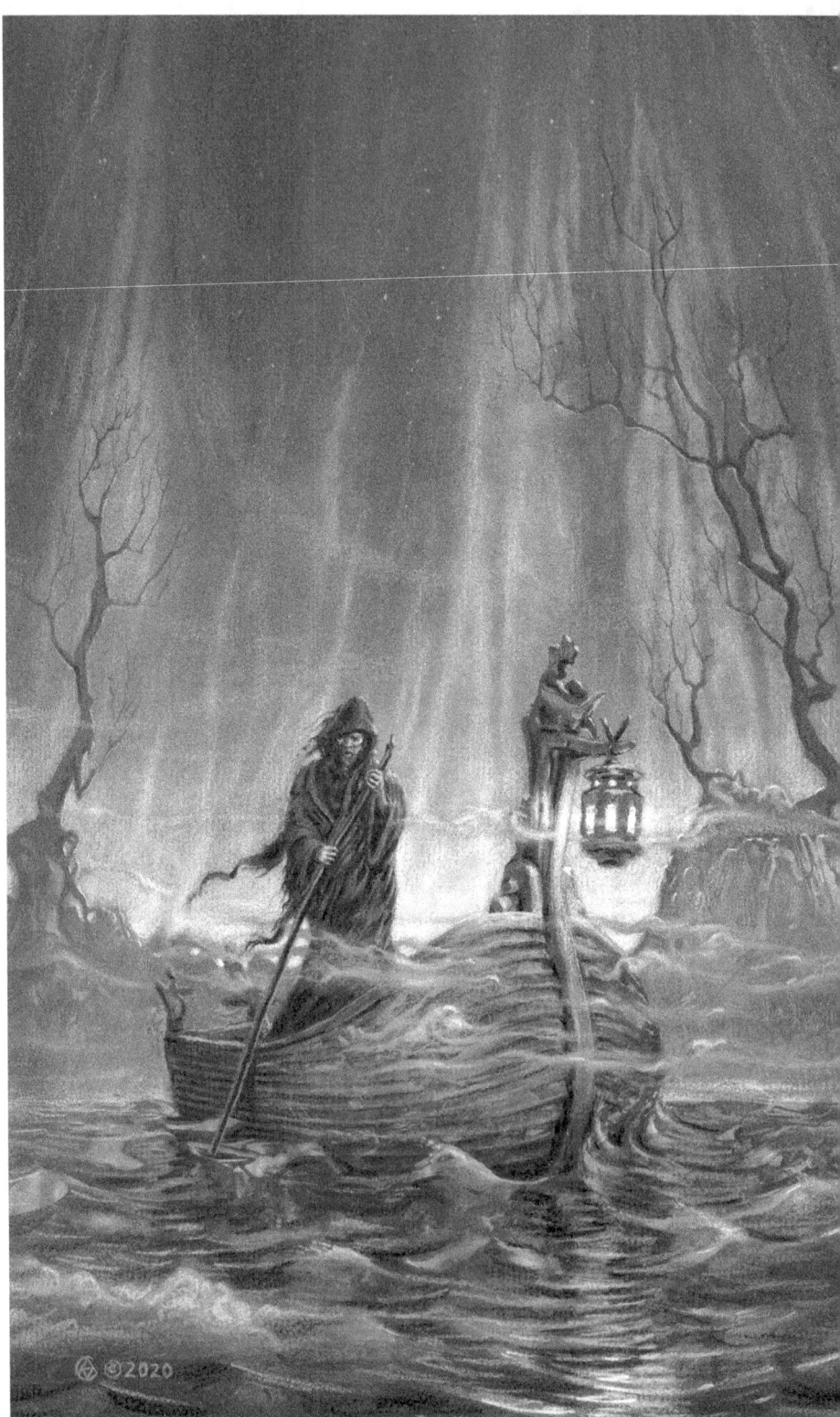

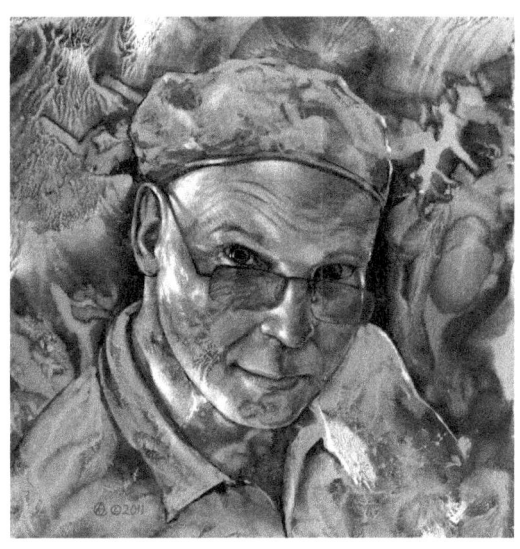

About the Author/Illustrator

Alan M. Clark hails from Tennessee, where he grew up in a house full of human bones and old medical books. At present, he lives in Eugene, Oregon with his wife, Melody. In his 35 year freelance career, he has created illustrations for hundreds of books, including works of fiction of various genres, nonfiction, textbooks, young adult fiction, and children's books. He is the author of 20 books, including twelve novels, a lavishly illustrated novella, four collections of fiction, one full-color book of his artwork, and two books of his monochrome artwork. The World Fantasy Award and four Chesley Awards are among the honors he's received for his work. Mr. Clark's company, IFD Publishing, has released 48 titles in various editions that include hardcovers, paperbacks, ebooks, and audio books. IFD Publishing's authors include F. Paul Wilson, Elizabeth Engstrom, and Jeremy Robert Johnson.

Connect with the Author Online

You can email the author or find out more about him through the following websites:

http://www.ifdpublishing.com
http://www.smashwords.com/profile/view/IFDPublishing

IFD Publishing Paperbacks

Novels:
Of Thimble and Threat, by Alan M. Clark
Baggage Check, by Elizabeth Engstrom
Bull's Labyrinth, by Eric Witchey
The Surgeon's Mate: A Dismemoir, by Alan M. Clark
Siren Promised, by Jeremy Robert Johnson and Alan M. Clark
Say Anything but Your Prayers, by Alan M. Clark
Candyland, by Elizabeth Engstrom
Apologies to the Cat's Meat Man, by Alan M. Clark
Lizzie Borden, by Elizabeth Engstrom
A Parliament of Crows, by Alan M. Clark
Lizard Wine, by Elizabeth Engstrom
The Door that Faced West, by Alan M. Clark
The Northwoods Chronicles, by Elizabeth Engstrom
The Prostitute's Price, by Alan M. Clark
The Assassin's Coin, by John Linwood Grant
13 Miller's Court, by Alan M. Clark and John Linwood Grant
Guys Named Bob, by Elizabeth Engstrom

Novelettes:
Mudlarks and the Silent Highwayman, by Alan M. Clark

Collections:
Professor Witchey's Miracle Mood Cure, by Eric Witchey

Nonfiction:
How to Write a Sizzling Sex Scene, by Elizabeth Engstrom
Divorce by Grand Canyon, by Elizabeth Engstrom

Art Books:
Full color:
The Paint in My Blood, Illustration and Fine Art, by Alan M. Clark
Black and white
Bastards and Guttersnipes, the Neglected Children of Alan M. Clark, Volume I
Bastards and Guttersnipes, the Neglected Children of Alan M. Clark, Volume II

IFD Publishing EBooks

(You can find the following titles at most distribution points for all ereading platforms.)

Novels:
The Prostitute's Price, by Alan M. Clark
The Assassin's Coin, by John Linwood Grant
13 Miller's Court, by Alan M. Clark and John Linwood Grant
Guys Named Bob, by Elizabeth Engstrom
Apologies to the Cat's Meat Man, by Alan M. Clark
Bull's Labyrinth, by Eric Witchey
The Surgeon's Mate: A Dismemoir, by Alan M. Clark
York's Moon, by Elizabeth Engstrom
Beyond the Serpent's Heart, by Eric Witchey
Lizzie Borden, by Elizabeth Engstrom
A Parliament of Crows, by Alan M. Clark
Lizard Wine, by Elizabeth Engstrom
Northwoods Chronicles, by Elizabeth Engstrom
Siren Promised, by Alan M. Clark and Jeremy Robert Johnson
To Kill a Common Loon, by Mitch Luckett
The Man in the Loon, by Mitch Luckett
Jack the Ripper Victim Series: Of Thimble and Threat by Alan M. Clark
Jack the Ripper Victim Series: The Double Event (includes two novels from the series: *Of Thimble and Threat* and *Say Anything But Your Prayers*) by Alan M. Clark
Candyland, by Elizabeth Engstrom
The Blood of Father Time: Book 1, The New Cut, by Alan M. Clark, Stephen C. Merritt & Lorelei Shannon
The Blood of Father Time: Book 2, The Mystic Clan's Grand Plot, by Alan M. Clark, Stephen C. Merritt & Lorelei Shannon
How I Met My Alien Bitch Lover: Book 1 from the Sunny World Inquisition Daily Letter Archives, by Eric Witchey
Baggage Check, by Elizabeth Engstrom
D. D. Murphry, Secret Policeman, by Alan M. Clark and Elizabeth Massie
Black Leather, by Elizabeth Engstrom

Novelettes:
The Tao of Flynn, by Eric Witchey
To Build a Boat, Listen to Trees, by Eric Witchey
Mudlarks and the Silent Highwayman, by Alan M. Clark

Children's Illustrated:
The Christmas Thingy, by F. Paul Wilson. Illustrated by Alan M. Clark

Collections:
Suspicions, by Elizabeth Engstrom
Professor Witchey's Miracle Mood Cure, by Eric Witchey

Short Fiction:
"Brittle Bones and Old Rope," by Alan M. Clark
"Crosley," by Elizabeth Engstrom
"The Apple Sniper," by Eric Witchey

Nonfiction:
How to Write a Sizzling Sex Scene, by Elizabeth Engstrom
Divorce by Grand Canyon, by Elizabeth Engstrom

IFD Publishing Audio Books

Novels:
The Door That Faced West by Alan M. Clark, read by Charles Hinckley
Jack the Ripper Victim Series: Of Thimble and Threat, by Alan M. Clark, read by Alicia Rose
Jack the Ripper Victim Series: Say Anything But Your Prayers, by Alan M. Clark, read by Alicia Rose
Jack the Ripper Victim Series: The Double Event by Alan M. Clark, read by Alicia Rose (includes two novels from the series: *Of Thimble and Threat* and *Say Anything But Your Prayers*)
A Parliament of Crows by Alan M. Clark, read by Laura Jennings
A Brutal Chill in August by Alan M. Clark, read by Alicia Rose
The Surgeon's Mate: A Dismemoir, by Alan M. Clark, read by Alan M. Clark
Apologies to the Cat's Meat Man, by Alan M. Clark, read by Alicia Rose
The Prostitute's Price, by Alan M. Clark, read by Alicia Rose
The Assassin's Coin, by John Linwood Grant, read by Alicia Rose
13 Miller's Court, by Alan M. Clark and John Linwood Grant, read by Alicia Rose

www.ingramcontent.com/pod-product-compliance
Lightning Source LLC
Chambersburg PA
CBHW071419220526
45469CB00004B/1346